Early
Literacy
Instruction
IN KINDERGARTEN

LORI JAMISON ROG

REGINA PUBLIC SCHOOLS
REGINA, SASKATCHEWAN, CANADA

INTERNATIONAL
Reading
Association

800 Barksdale Road, PO Box 8139
Newark, Delaware 19714-8139, USA
www.reading.org

The International Reading Association attempts, through its publications, to provide a forum for a wide spectrum of opinions on reading. This policy permits divergent viewpoints without implying the endorsement of the Association.

Director of Publications   Joan M. Irwin
Editorial Director, Books and Special Projects   Matthew W. Baker
Senior Editor, Books and Special Projects   Tori Mello Bachman
Permissions Editor   Janet S. Parrack
Production Editor   Shannon Benner
Assistant Editor   Corinne M. Mooney
Editorial Assistant   Tyanna L. Collins
Publications Manager   Beth Doughty
Production Department Manager   Iona Sauscermen
Supervisor, Electronic Publishing   Anette Schütz-Ruff
Senior Electronic Publishing Specialist   Cheryl J. Strum
Electronic Publishing Specialist   R. Lynn Harrison
Proofreader   Charlene M. Nichols

Project Editor   Janet S. Parrack

Photo Credits   Cover and interior photos from EyeWire, Inc.

Library of Congress Cataloging-in-Publication Data
Rog, Lori J. (Lori Jamison)
    Early literacy instruction in kindergarten / Lori J. Rog.
        p.   cm.
Includes bibliographical references and index.
ISBN 0-87207-169-3 (pbk. : alk. paper)
    1. Reading (Kindergarten)   2. Language arts (Kindergarten)
3. Kindergarten—Activity programs.   I. Title.
LB1181.2.R64   2001
372.6—dc21   2001003257

Contents

Acknowledgments

I would like to thank the teachers and students of Regina Public Schools, from whom I am constantly learning. In particular, I am grateful to Connie Watson for her valuable ideas and to Sharlene Kujat, Marion Gorrie, Joanne Zepp, Jackie Pawson, and Joyce Allen for suggesting literature selections for this book.

I am also grateful to Dr. Sandra Blenkinsop at the University of Regina for her support during this project, as well as to Dr. Mary Cronin and Dr. Kathryn McNaughton for their suggestions and questions.

Most of all, I would like to thank Paul for his loving treatment of my writing and of me.

This book is dedicated to Jennifer, who taught me how children learn to read when she was in kindergarten.

PART I

The Exemplary Kindergarten Classroom

CHAPTER 1

The Importance of Early Literacy Instruction in Kindergarten

Each fall, millions of kindergarten children start school, embarking on a learning adventure that will take 13 years or more, involving dozens of teachers and many different classrooms, with experiences the effects of which will last a lifetime. Their first foray into formal education all begins on that first day, with a tearful goodbye to mom. That first day, first month, and first year are all crucial. As so many educators know, a child's experience in kindergarten lays the groundwork for continuing social, emotional, and cognitive development throughout the school years. For us as teachers, the message is obvious: We must make that first year an experience that is warm with love, busy with activity, and rich with meaning.

When asked why they go to school, some children might tell you that it is to play with other kids or get a good job when they grow up. Some will tell you that they want to learn to count, or print their names, or pet the classroom hamster. But most children will reply that they go to school to learn to read. Literacy development, in the eyes of both students and the general public, is one of the most important functions schools serve. For some children, the school experience will be a further extension of an already rich relationship with print begun long before they enter the classroom. Others will depend on school almost entirely to open the doors to language and literature. Either way, the goals are clear. In kindergarten, the teacher must take a group of children with highly disparate literacy skills and bring them all to the world of print, to an understanding of some of the basic concepts in reading, and to a point where they begin to master the skills and attitudes that will make them lifelong readers.

> *"The richness and quality of the experiences encountered in Kindergarten contribute to the child's development as a lifelong learner."*
> **(Gatzke, 1991, p. 97)**

The International Reading Association (IRA) and the National Association for the Education of Young Children (NAEYC) believe that the main goals of literacy development in kindergarten are for children to "develop basic concepts of print and begin to engage in and experiment with reading and writing" (IRA/NAEYC, 1998, p. 200). Yet the means to this end are as diverse as the people who practice them, and there is probably no greater diversity of instructional practice at any other grade level than in kindergarten. For example, let us take a peek into two kindergarten classrooms in the same school:

• •

Mrs. Reid views the role of kindergarten as preparing children for the demands of academic instruction in Grade 1. Her students are involved in a variety of activities, but spend some time each day completing "reading readiness" activities such as reciting letter-sound correspondences, completing left-to-right directionality tasks, and tracing alphabet letters for correct formation.

On the other hand, her colleague, Ms. Drew, is very proud of her play-oriented classroom. Her classroom buzzes with students involved in a variety of activities from puzzles to dress-ups to carpentry. Books and pencils are available, but no specific attention is drawn to them. Ms. Drew believes that the children will use these materials when they are ready. She views the role of kindergarten as developing students' confidence in themselves as learners, rather than offering formal instruction.

Because Mrs. Reid believes that kindergarten is primarily preparation for Grade 1, her focus is on skill-development activities. She follows a model popular in the 1950s and 1960s in which actual reading of books and stories must be preceded by specific prereading activities. Ms. Drew, on the other hand, draws her ideas from a more play-oriented philosophy, which originated in the 1970s. Print materials are available, but reading and writing are neither taught nor expected. Ms. Drew believes that children will access text spontaneously when ready, so books are available in class, but the reading experience itself is not specifically fostered.

• •

Mrs. Reid and Ms. Drew clearly represent opposite ends of the spectrum of teaching practices in kindergarten. In between, there are almost as many kinds of programs and practices as there are kindergarten teachers. The question remains, however: Which teaching practices are best for early reading development among kindergarten children?

How Children Learn

Today, we know much more about how children learn than ever before. Both research and practice confirm that, although not all children develop at the same time and rate, most children go through a similar sequence of developmental stages as they grow. For example, we know that children will sit before they stand and stand before they walk. We accept that there is gradual progress in physical development and that skills will improve with maturity. In the same way, intellectual growth develops gradually over time, but follows predictable patterns and stages.

Children are active learners who construct their own understandings about the world as they experience new things and interact with others. Jean Piaget was among the first to theorize that learning involves constantly creating and testing ideas about how the world works. As new experiences challenge these ideas, learners must either assimilate them into their existing knowledge banks or refine their existing knowledge to accommodate the new information.

When a child begins to talk, he learns very quickly what sounds generate praise and results. He may find that sounds like "wa" or "wawa" produce not only delight on the part of his parents, but a drink of water as well. So he assimilates these sounds into his existing repertoire of language. On the other hand, he may find that "gaga," while equally delightful, does not result in a drink of water or anything else. He, therefore, must change his mind-set to accommodate this new knowledge.

Children use the same processes as they learn about written language. Long before they are able to recognize actual words, they role-play reading, using illustrations and their own repertoire of language and experience to tell the story in a book (Sulzby, 1985). In writing, children begin to experiment with squiggles, which gradually become symbols and letter-like forms before they can print conventional alphabet letters (Clay, 1975).

Learning to talk may seem like the most natural process in the world. But as children experiment with oral language, they constantly receive feedback, both incidental and intentional. In the same way, it is not enough to simply surround children with books and assume that they will learn to read and write. It is the process of modeling and feedback that creates readers:

> Although it may seem as though some children acquire these understandings magically, or on their own, studies suggest that they are the beneficiaries of considerable, though playful and informal, adult guidance and instruction. (IRA/NAEYC, 1998, p. 198)

The interactions around print with adults and other significant people in their lives have a great impact on children's literacy development (Hiebert & Raphael, 1998). Among those significant people are their kindergarten teachers. This is why the kindergarten program must provide not only a print-rich environment, but also carefully organized learning experiences. In the two vignettes presented earlier, we can see that Ms. Drew's play-oriented classroom offers incidental literacy experiences, but her focus on unstructured activity may not provide the foundations many children need for learning to read and write. On the other hand, Mrs. Reid's emphasis on skill mastery may undermine both the developmental nature of learning and the diversity of her students. Although students may learn some literacy basics, they may miss opportunities to construct their own ideas about the world through playful interaction with print and with others.

What Is an Exemplary Kindergarten Program?

We know that an effective kindergarten program provides both a print-rich play environment and carefully organized learning experiences. It is structured in such a way as to respect the learning processes of each student and help them reach their full potential. It acknowledges that all children will be at different stages of development and require different instructional strategies. And, at its heart is a teacher who has thorough knowledge of the curriculum, the learning process, and the children involved. With this knowledge, the teacher can set appropriate learning goals to meet the needs of her students. It is these challenging but achievable goals that are the essence of a developmentally appropriate program (IRA/NAEYC, 1998).

In the following chapters, we explore the elements of an exemplary kindergarten literacy program. In the first section of this book, we examine the concept of "developmental appropriateness" and discuss the research on what children in kindergarten should know and be able to do. We will look at how to organize the kindergarten classroom and those elements that are essential to an effective program.

The second section of the book presents strategies for literacy instruction in kindergarten. Interactive read-alouds, shared reading, independent reading, modeled writing, independent writing, and language play combine to form a balanced literacy program that promotes both skill development and desire to read. In closing, we reflect on the increasing diversity of students in our classrooms, and how to both honor and accommodate that diversity.

CHAPTER 2

Developmentally Appropriate Literacy Instruction: A Contradiction in Terms?

If there is a buzzword in early literacy instruction today, it is *developmentally appropriate*. This term has been used to justify a range of pedagogical practices in kindergarten and preschool classrooms, from free-play programs to using highly structured baby basals.

Developmentally appropriate practices may be described as procedures and routines that are consistent with children's natural course of development. Just as physical growth is developmental, so is intellectual growth. Although most children pass through similar phases en route to independence, we know that they will not reach each stage at the same time or at the same rate. The teacher's job is to set challenging but attainable learning goals for her students, based on her assessment of what they know and can do, and then to support and guide them as they progress toward those goals. These goals form the core of the developmentally appropriate curriculum (IRA/NAEYC, 1998).

It seems, however, that the term *developmentally appropriate* means different things to different people. In some cases, it seems to have joined the many other maligned and misunderstood terms such as *whole language* and *balanced literacy*. Some teachers have interpreted developmentally appropriate to be simply establishing conditions that nurture healthy emotional, social, and cognitive growth, and waiting for learning to occur naturally, without intervention or instruction. In these classrooms, reading and writing are often perceived as "academic skills" that do not belong in child-centered early childhood programs (McGill-Franzen, 1992, p. 57). These teachers question whether there is a place for purposeful, systematic instruction in the developmentally appropriate curriculum. Is the phrase "developmentally appropriate instruction" a contradiction in terms?

Reading Readiness: A Historical Perspective

Direct instruction historically has played a key role in early childhood classrooms. Until recently, a "reading readiness" philosophy dominated early literacy instruction, part of a belief that progress in motor or cognitive skill was the result of "neural ripening," with behaviors unfolding naturally as children reached a certain age (Teale & Sulzby, 1986, p. ix). The concept of reading readiness was based on the premise that there was an appropriate "mental age" at which children would naturally learn to read and, until they reached this point, involvement in reading and writing activities was regarded as "futile or even deleterious" (Hiebert & Raphael, 1998, p. 5). That magical moment of readiness was determined to be age 6 years, 6 months, based on the results of the 1931 reading assessments in Winnetka, Illinois, USA (Morphett & Washburne, 1931, in McGill-Franzen, 1992).

It became necessary, then, to find teaching and learning activities for the first half of Grade 1 that would not interfere with natural maturational processes; in other words, that would not directly involve reading and writing. Visual and auditory discrimination exercises, tracking, matching letters and sounds, and naming strings of letters all were identified as reading readiness activities. Children were not given books to read until these discrete skills were mastered.

During the 1960s, more attention began to be paid to infancy and early childhood development. In 1967, Marie Clay conducted an extensive study of the early reading behaviors of 5-year-old kindergarten children in New Zealand, finding that even young children could engage in some reading behaviors, such as "visual sensitivity to letter and word forms, appropriate directional movements, self-correction and synchronized matching of spoken word units with written word units" (Teale & Sulzby, 1987, p. xv).

Clay's and other studies of literacy development in early childhood (Harste, Woodward, & Burke, 1984; Teale & Sulzby, 1986) postulated that literacy development begins long before children start formal instruction. In her 1966 doctoral dissertation, Clay coined the term *emergent literacy* to define the ongoing and developmental process of understanding and using written language from birth until independence (Morrow, Strickland, & Woo, 1998). Furthermore, she asserted that "attention to the formal properties of print and correspondence with sound is the final step in a progression, not the entry point to understanding what written language is" (Clay, 1991, p. 33). This contradicted a long-standing belief that knowledge of letter-sound correspondences was the starting point for reading.

Emergent Literacy: What We Know Now

We now recognize that children know about and participate in the functions of literacy long before they can discriminate between letters or recognize correspondences between letters and sounds. Literacy is developing from the time that a child recognizes that the golden arches represent a fast food chain or that the octagonal red sign tells Mom to stop the car. Children as young as 3 years old can identify labels from familiar products such as toothpaste, fast food, and snacks (Harste, Woodward, & Burke, 1984), and it is not uncommon to see lists, letters, stories, and maps created by children who are not yet in school.

Literacy is also developing when a child insists that the scribbles on his paper say, "Grandma is coming," or "This is what I want Santa to bring." When a child recognizes that symbols can have meaning, he has tools for reading. When he uses symbols to represent his ideas, he is a writer. In fact, Neuman and Roskos (1998) suggest that the term *emergent* may be inappropriate, because it implies that literacy has a beginning point. They suggest that *early literacy* is a more suitable term to describe a process that is "ongoing and continuous throughout a lifetime" (p. 2).

Most children go through similar stages as they develop reading and writing proficiency (IRA/NAEYC, 1998). However, not all children reach each phase of development at the same time and pace. Early experiences with print play a significant role in literacy development (Adams, 1991), both in determining a child's literacy level when entering kindergarten and in defining attitudes toward reading and learning.

Meet Dakota and Michael, two children who attend the same kindergarten class, but come from quite different literacy backgrounds:

• •

Dakota lives with her grandmother in a small house not far from the school. Dakota's grandmother works long hours as a cashier at the local supermarket and has little time for reading and writing. Occasionally, when she's not too tired, she will tell Dakota a traditional story at bedtime. Most of the time, Dakota and her grandmother watch television together.

Michael attends the same school as Dakota. Michael's father, a professor, and his mother, an artist, fill their home with books. They make regular trips to the library, where Michael knows how to find his favorite books. Michael often sees his mother and father reading and writing, both for professional and recreational purposes.

• •

Although virtually all children in our society are surrounded by environmental print, some children come to school with a great deal more knowledge about how print works than others do. In fact, researchers like Marilyn

Adams (1990) suggest that children like Michael have an advantage of over 1,000 hours more experiences with print before starting school than children like Dakota. Although it may seem that these children acquire literacy understandings simply by immersion in print, in reality they have usually received a great deal of informal instruction and guidance from parents and other significant people in their lives (IRA/NAEYC, 1998). In fact, Delores Durkin's (1966) classic research of children who learned to read before coming to school revealed certain patterns in their home literacy experiences. She found that when the parents of these children read books aloud, they would discuss the story, point out words and other features of print, respond to the child's questions, and share in various other literacy activities such as letter writing and noting environmental print.

The interactions with others around print have the greatest impact on literacy development (Hiebert & Raphael, 1998). Therefore, it is important for both teachers and parents to be active participants in their children's literacy development. According to IRA and NAEYC, "failing to give children literacy experiences until they are school-age can severely limit the reading and writing levels they ultimately attain" (IRA/NAEYC, 1998, p. 197).

The report of the National Reading Panel (2000) recommends that systematic literacy instruction begin as early as possible, particularly for those children whose home environments do not facilitate literacy development. The IRA/NAEYC position statement (1998) states further that "the ability to read and write does not develop naturally without careful planning and instruction" (p. 197).

Therefore, the question is not whether we *should* provide systematic literacy instruction in a developmentally appropriate program, but *what* that literacy instruction should look like.

What Do Good Teachers Do?

By definition, developmental learning means that each child will progress at his or her own rate. It is important to respect those individual differences and to set challenging but achievable learning goals for each child to help him or her reach the next phase of development. This is the role of the teacher. An effective teacher of early literacy

- understands and acknowledges the developmental nature of literacy learning,
- expects all children to achieve success,
- accepts individual differences and rates of progress, and

- provides scaffolded instruction to help each student reach the next level of independence. (IRA, 2000)

The concept of scaffolding was based on the research of Russian psychologist Lev Vygotsky (1978), who theorized that there is a zone of proximal development between what a child can do independently and what he or she is able to do with the assistance of someone more knowledgeable or skilled. By talking with grownups and capable peers as they go about doing the things literate people do, children are able to construct meanings for things they could not otherwise understand on their own. The role of scaffolded instruction is to "move ahead of development and pull it along" (McGill-Franzen, 1992, p. 58). Just as scaffolding serves as a temporary support for the construction worker to reach heights he is unable to reach on his own, scaffolded instruction extends children's development so that tomorrow they are able to do on their own what they could only do with assistance today.

It is important that early literacy instruction offer "rich demonstrations, interactions, and independent explorations" (Strickland & Morrow, 1989, p. 6) that provide children with opportunities to experiment with reading and writing, to interact with one another as they explore and learn about written language, and to receive teacher guidance as they progress from one level of independence to the next.

Most importantly, the developmentally appropriate program is one in which the teacher has carefully considered both the psychological and the physical environment and established a climate in which children are not expected to progress at the same time or pace. Approximations are considered to be signs of growth rather than cause for concern (Brewer, 1998). In any kindergarten class, one is likely to find students who have had several years of organized preschool experience and others who may never have held a pencil or a book before coming to school.

Unfortunately, according to the IRA/NAEYC position statement (1998), outdated and developmentally inappropriate practices are still prevalent in many classrooms (see Figure 1). An understanding of emergent literacy theory and developmentally appropriate practice reveals that

> Every kindergarten child is entitled to a balanced instructional program that includes daily experiences of being read to and independently reading meaningful and engaging stories and informational texts; daily opportunities and teacher support to do many kinds of writing for different purposes; and extensive opportunities to work in small groups for focused instruction and collaboration with other children. (Adapted from IRA/NAEYC, 1998)

> priorities are out of balance and out of keeping with the nature of young children as
> literacy learners when kindergarten and readiness programs concentrate on letter-

Figure 1
What Developmentally Appropriate Is and Is Not

Developmentally Appropriate Literacy Practices in Kindergarten	Developmentally Inappropriate Literacy Practices in Kindergarten
The curriculum is integrated so that children's learning occurs primarily through projects and learning centers that teachers plan and that reflect children's interests and suggestions.	The curriculum is divided into separate subjects, and time is allotted for each.
Children have opportunities to work alone or in groups on self-selected learning activities with many opportunities for socialization and collaborative problem solving.	Children are expected to work individually and silently on most learning activities.
The classroom environment is designed to allow children to learn through active involvement with one other.	Students spend a great deal of time completing worksheets and other seatwork.
Play centers are enriched with literacy artifacts (paper, pencils, and books) that enable children to learn actively and socially with others.	Play centers are available only for children who finish their seatwork early. Little attention is paid to integrating literacy activities into all learning centers.
Learning materials and activities are concrete, real, and relevant to children's lives.	Materials are limited primarily to books, workbooks, and pencils.
The goals of the language program are for children to expand their ability to communicate orally and through reading and writing.	The goal of the language program is for children to acquire readiness skills to prepare them for learning to read and write.

Adapted from the *NAEYC Position Statement on Developmentally Appropriate Practices in the Primary Grades Serving 5- Through 8-Year Olds*, 1986.

sound matching, letter discrimination and letter names, and give only scant attention to activities that involve children with stories.

(Teale & Sulzby, 1986, p. 6).

Everything we know about how children learn reinforces the importance of the teacher in developmentally appropriate early literacy instruction. Teachers must set challenging but attainable literacy goals for their students based on their understandings of child development, knowledge of the curriculum, and familiarity with their students. They must select motivating and appropriate learning activities based on ongoing and current knowledge of the research on effective instruction. And of course, they must know their students in order to design a suitable classroom program. The skilled teacher must have a comprehensive understanding of curriculum, the learning process, and the children themselves. She constantly must update her knowledge of current research and pedagogy. Most important, she knows that there is no single method or approach that will work best for all children. Knowledgeable and effective teachers are part of every effective classroom. They are the heart of the developmentally appropriate program.

For Further Reading

Learning to Read and Write: Developmentally Appropriate Practices for Young Children. (1998). A Joint Position Statement of the International Reading Association (IRA) and the National Association for the Education of Young Children (NAEYC).

CHAPTER 3

What Do Kindergarten Children Need to Know?

Children enter kindergarten with a wide range of experiences with literacy and print. Some have had a rich home experience full of books, stories, and reading games. Others will still be struggling with English as a second language or will have seen few children's books of any kind. In fact, the developmental levels of the students in a kindergarten class are likely to represent an age range of up to 5 years (IRA/NAEYC, 1998).

> *"The main goal for kindergarten is for children to develop basic concepts of print and begin to engage in and experiment with reading and writing."*
> **(IRA/NAEYC, 1998, p. 200)**

Although individual objectives will vary with each child, there are certain general goals toward which teachers strive as they prepare kindergarten students for first grade. In order to lay the foundation for success in learning to read and write, children must develop the following critical understandings in kindergarten (Hall & Cunningham, 1997):

- They must learn the conventions and structures of spoken language and add many new words and concepts to their speaking vocabularies.

- They must develop the awareness that words are made up of sounds, otherwise known as phonological awareness.

- They must learn certain concepts about print, such as the fact that English text is read left-to-right and top-to-bottom.

- They must learn letter names and sounds in the context of meaningful words.

- They must learn that text follows different forms such as stories, signs or messages, and serves different functions.

- They must learn that reading provides enjoyment and information, and ultimately develop the desire to read and write for themselves.

Oral Language and Vocabulary Development

A strong oral language base is always the foundation for learning to read. Most early readers cannot read words that are not in their speaking vocabularies. Knowledge of how language works and how words go together helps children decode unfamiliar words. Through listening to and participating in conversations, and by asking questions and hearing answers, children learn about language and about the world.

Oral language development has four separate but interactive components: function, content, form, and sound structure. Each works together to help the speaker communicate in a clear, effective, and grammatically correct manner.

Function

The language that we use differs according to the circumstances, audience, and purposes for which it is intended. This is the function of language, also known as pragmatics. We speak differently when we are talking to an infant than when we are presenting a paper at a university or delivering a toast at a wedding. As adults, we are accustomed to changes in language, style, and address. But these subtleties often are not evident to children.

The social conventions of language need to be explicitly modeled and taught, beginning in kindergarten. Some of these conventions include the type of language used: formal or slang, passionate or calm, complex or simple, and even such body language as gestures or the distance one speaker stands from another.

Different cultures have different language conventions, and simple gestures or tones of voice may be interpreted in diverse ways. Some children may find the differences between the informal communication styles of the home ("Go get a book") and the more formal language patterns of school ("Allison, will you please get a book from the bookshelf?") very difficult to fathom. Teachers must be sensitive to the language and cultural patterns that their students bring to school. Formal patterns of language are not necessarily better, but they are different. Children may need help to develop the flexibility that enables them to adapt to differing communication patterns.

Students in kindergarten must learn that spoken communication changes according to the situation and the purposes for which it is used. Vocabulary, tone of voice, and gestures used on the playground are not likely to be appropriate when speaking to the teacher in the classroom. In the same way, the language of books is different from spoken language, and it is different for particular purposes. Books that provide information use a different language and structure than books that are intended to entertain. When children understand the pragmatics of oral and written language, they are better able to predict and create meaning when reading and writing.

Content and Form

Content, or semantics, refers to the meaning of words. Before they can begin to read, students must have a repertoire of words in their speaking vocabularies. They must not only know and be able to use a bank of words, but also understand relationships between words, multiple meanings (for example, the word *set* has 18 dictionary definitions), and the nuances of tone (the difference between "Go to the office now!" and "Please drop by the office when you have time"). Language is a self-extending system; as children learn language, they create structures to learn more language. The more children talk, the more they learn to talk.

Form, or syntax, refers to the conventions that govern how words go together in our language. Formal grammar and sentence structure are aspects of syntax. A knowledge of oral language syntax helps readers predict unfamiliar vocabulary by giving them a sense of how the word fits into the sentence.

By the time children reach kindergarten, they are able to use appropriate language forms most of the time, although some irregular forms may cause them problems, such as "I brang it," or "I goed there." This is most effectively taught and reinforced by plenty of modeling and exposure to formal language structures in dialogue and in books. When children are read to regularly and frequently, they also learn that language structures in books may be quite different from oral language structures. This is another important stepping stone to literacy development.

Classic research by Cambourne (1988) defines the relationship between oral language development and literacy learning. He outlines what are popularly known as "Cambourne's Conditions," under which language learning is supported:

1. Immersion in language

2. Demonstrations of literate behavior

3. Expectation that students will be able to succeed

4. Responsibility on the part of the learner

5. Encouragement of approximation as learning is constructed

6. Recognition that there is some use or purpose in the learning

7. Positive responses to student learning

8. Engagement of the learner

Sound Structure

Words are made up of sounds. An understanding of sound structures is more than correct pronunciation. Understanding sound structures enables the young reader to sound out words and to make predictions based on knowledge of how sounds are combined in words.

Evaluating Oral Language and Vocabulary Development

At home, children learn to talk. At school they must also talk to learn. Schools must help children develop the vocabulary they need to express their ideas and questions as well as an understanding of the sounds and structures of our language. Modeling of adult speech, opportunities to talk with others, and frequent exposure to books help most children develop these important concepts. In assessing a child's oral language skills, the teacher should consider the following:

Behaviors

- Uses appropriate volume and tone of voice
- Knows how to take turns when speaking
- Stays on topic
- Asks questions
- Seems to pay attention when another person is speaking

Vocabulary

- Can name colors, numbers, and names of familiar objects
- Uses vocabulary appropriately for purpose and audience
- Is able to retell parts or all of a story read aloud
- Understands and uses prepositions such as *under*, *over*, *in*, and *beside*
- Understands directions

Language Structures

- Can use connectors such as *and*, *so*, *because*, and *if*
- Often speaks in complete sentences
- Generally speaks with grammatical correctness

Speech Sounds

- Articulates speech sounds correctly
- Speaks clearly and fluently

Phonological Awareness

Phonological awareness is the understanding that words are made up of sounds. The largest and most easily recognized sound components in words are syllables. Most children can hear that the word *happy* has two parts, or that *book* has one.

The smallest units of sound that can change the meaning of a word are called *phonemes*. Usually phonemes are associated with individual letters such as /m/ or combinations such as /th/. *Rimes* and *onsets* are also sound chunks. The onset is the initial consonant or consonant cluster that begins a syllable. The rime is the vowel and any consonants that come after it. For example, in the word *start*, the onset is /st/ and the rime is /art/. When words share the same rime, such as *cart* and *smart*, they rhyme.

Often the term *phonological awareness* is used interchangeably with the more specific term *phonemic awareness*. Phonemic awareness refers to an ability to hear and manipulate phonemes. Phonological awareness is a more inclusive term that encompasses larger units of sound such as syllables and rhymes as well as phonemes.

Phonological awareness is an oral language skill. It deals with the ability to hear and manipulate the sounds in words and is not explicitly connected to letters and print. Most researchers agree that phonemic awareness abilities in kindergarten are a good predictor of successful reading acquisition later on (Adams, 1990; IRA, 1998; Stanovich, 1993/1994). However, some phonological awareness skills precede conventional reading, some develop at the same time, and others are acquired as the result of an ability to read (see Figure 2).

The most basic level of phonological awareness—perception of rhyme—develops earliest and most easily. This has led some researchers to believe that an understanding of and ability to segment words into rimes and onsets is a precursor to reading (Goswami & Bryant, 1990). Intermediate-level skills such as phoneme segmentation and blending have a strong reciprocal relationship with reading. It is likely that they develop along with reading ability and facilitate decoding and spelling (Nation & Hulme, 1997).

> Phonemic awareness is not phonics. Phonemic awareness is an understanding about the structures and patterns of spoken language. Phonics, on the other hand, refers to the connection between letters and spoken sounds.

Highest-level phonological awareness tasks, such as phoneme deletion and manipulation, are generally unattainable by children who have received no formal reading instruction (Adams, 1990; Peterson & Haines, 1998). Think about the mental processes involved in removing the /st/ from *star* and replacing it with /f/ to make *far*. According to Adams (1990), the ability to delete a phoneme from a word, insert a new one, and put the word back together is virtually impossible without well-developed literacy skills.

Adams, Foorman, Lundberg, and Beeler (1998) attest that, "research clearly shows that phonemic awareness can be developed through instruction, and…doing so significantly accelerates reading and writing achievement" (p. 3). However, it is important that this instruction be just one part of the overall literacy program.

Figure 2
Levels of Phonological Awareness Tasks

1. Recognition of Rhyme and Alliteration	Which words start the same: *car, cat, lock*? Which word doesn't belong: *pin, tip, fin*?	The ability to focus on which elements of sound make words sound the same or different is an important precursor to reading.
2. Phoneme Blending and Syllable Splitting	What word do you get when you blend together /m/.../a/.../p/? What is left when you take the /p/ off of *pink*?	These abilities to blend sounds and to isolate rimes and onsets are likely to develop along with reading ability; each supports the development of the other.
3. Phoneme Segmentation and Manipulation	How many sounds do you hear in *tent*? What word do you have when you replace the /a/ in *pat* with an /i/?	These advanced skills probably develop as a result of learning to read, as they are difficult to do without well-developed spelling skills.

Adapted from M. Adams, 1990

Most children develop phonemic awareness skills through language play. In fact, about 80% of children develop phonemic awareness without any explicit instruction (IRA/NAEYC, 1998). Many traditional home and school reading activities, such as reciting nursery rhymes, reading alphabet books, sharing poems and riddles, or singing songs, help to develop phonemic awareness by drawing children's attention to the sounds of language and manipulating sounds in a playful environment.

"Probably the most accessible, practical and useful vehicles to enhance students' sensitivity to the phonological basis of their language are children's books that deal playfully with speech sounds through rhyme, alliteration, assonance or other phoneme manipulation."
(Yopp, 1995, p. 538)

Some children, however, will require additional instruction, either as a result of learning difficulties or a lack of experience with print. For these children, manipulation of sounds must be made explicit and practiced. Although there is no consensus on the best way to teach phonological awareness, Braunger and Lewis (1997) note that effective practices include

- games that emphasize rhyming and the structure of words,
- drawing children's attention to letters and words in books and in the environment,
- opportunities to use invented spelling,
- language experience—dictation of children's own speech, and
- rich experiences with literature in shared reading experiences.

Concepts About Print

There seems to be a magic moment in literacy development when children realize that writing is talk written down. In truth, writing is much more complex than that, but that initial realization is wonderful indeed.

Concepts About Print

- **Pictures are different from text.**
- **Print is read from left to right.**
- **Oral language can be written down and then read aloud.**
- **Alphabet letters have names and represent sounds.**
- **Words are separated by spaces.**
- **English text starts at the top left-hand corner of the page.**

We know that oral language is supported by the context in which it is spoken, as well as by facial expression, gestures, and tone of voice. Written language does not have this support; that is why conventions such as punctuation are needed to show emphasis, pauses, and completion of thought. For kindergarten children, understanding the conventions of language, or concepts about print, is an important milestone on the literacy journey.

One of the first things kindergarten children learn as they experiment with letters and words is that print carries a message, and that there are certain consistencies about print (Lesiak, 1997). Print is print, whether it is written using a crayon or a paintbrush, whether it is scribbled on a wall, published in a book, or stenciled on a T-shirt. Print can appear by itself or with pictures. It can be handwritten, printed in italics, or ALL CAPS, and it still reads the same way. Some children appreciate this intuitively; for others it must be demonstrated.

Other conventions about English print go back to the origins of the language. For instance, English print is read from top to bottom, left to right, and pages in a book are read from front to back, not the other way around. Mastery of these basic concepts about print is essential to the development of reading proficiency (Clay, 1991). Again, many children pick these up by repeated exposure to print through reading, stories, and writing; for others these concepts should be taught.

Eventually, children must learn that print corresponds to speech, word by word. This is another developmental milestone. The problem, of course, is that we generally do not speak in individual words; we speak in streams of words. We say, "Dyuwannago t'th'store and geddavideo?" rather than enunciate "Do-you-want-to-go-to-the-store-and-get-a-video?" As they learn to interpret text, kindergarten children must develop the understanding of words as separate entities.

Letter Names and Sounds

When preschool children first begin to write, they do so in seemingly random scribbles. Yet, even at this stage, they are able to differentiate between the "writing" and the "picture," though this distinction may not always be evident to the casual observer (see Figure 3).

Later they begin to invent letter-like forms, which may include actual letters, numbers, and other recognizable symbols (see Figure 4). Kindergarten writers are likely to put marks on a page without intending any specific meaning in advance, then decide what the marks mean when the piece is complete. For example, when observed writing diligently, 5-year-old Mark was asked what he was writing. "I don't know," replied Mark, "I didn't draw the picture yet." At this stage, children realize that print symbols convey messages, but they do not yet understand that the symbols remain constant and convey the same message every time.

At some point, children discover that there is a connection between letters and the sounds of words; they may begin representing entire words with an initial consonant, later adding other consonants and finally vowels. When

Figure 3
Random Scribbles

"We went to the fire station. We climbed on the firetruck and we saw a real fire."

students start to represent the sounds they hear with alphabet letters, they are embarking on the adventure of invented spelling (see Figure 5).

Invented, temporary, or phonetic spelling is a critical practice in early writing and must be supported in the classroom. This is how children develop hypotheses about the way language goes together, then test and adjust those hypotheses based on subsequent experience (Clay, 1975).

Sulzby, Teale, and Kamberelis (1989) caution against the assumption that "children cannot write (that is, cannot compose) until they have mastered the mechanics, and that the only way they should write is through conventional orthography (p. 69)."

Figure 4
Letter-Like Forms

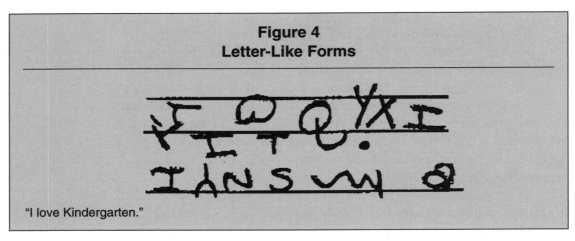

"I love Kindergarten."

Figure 5
Invented Spelling

"Mom's number book with love and kisses and hugs."

Of course, many children will not even use invented spelling in kindergarten; they will remain at the scribbling or random-letter stages. Sulzby (1992) also points out that the transition toward conventional literacy may be recursive rather than linear: Children often revert to previous stages or may function at different stages for different writing purposes. For example, the child who is writing wonderfully creative pieces in invented spelling may suddenly discover that there is a right way to spell words and begin limiting her vocabulary choice to words she knows how to spell conventionally.

Too many primary programs erroneously focus children's attention first and almost exclusively on form, introducing alphabet letters and practicing them for mastery before students are given opportunities to use these letters to express ideas (Casbergue, 1998). There is much more to literacy development than the ability to name alphabet letters or to write them correctly. Children need a rich literacy environment that also includes vocabulary development, sense of story, and conventions of print, as well as a chance to explore the ways in which scribbles develop into letters and letters develop into words. They need to see a meaningful purpose for alphabet letters, which is why they should be taught in the context of names and words that are significant to the children.

> **Invented, temporary, or phonetic spelling is a critical practice in early writing and must be supported in the classroom.**

There is substantial evidence to support a positive relationship between knowledge of letter names at the end of kindergarten and reading achievement in Grade 1 (IRA/NAEYC, 1998). However, efforts to replicate this research by focusing exclusively on letter-name instruction found that letter-naming drills alone, without immersing children in other literacy tasks, did not increase children's success of becoming literate (Blanchard & Logan, 1988, in Lesiak 1997; Samuels, 1973, in Hiebert & Raphael, 1998). We may surmise that children who come to school with a knowledge of letter names also have had a variety of other literacy experiences as well. Children need rich literacy experiences that will encourage them to learn the letters and letter sounds that make up reading.

A reasonable goal is for children to be able to recognize and name letters of the alphabet by the end of kindergarten. Certainly, knowing letter names aids understanding of the phonetic principle, because many letters "say" their own name. Twenty-two of the 26 letter names represent their corresponding sound, and many words also contain letter names within them (for example, *become* [b] or *are* [r]). When children are encouraged to form letters with clay or trace letters in finger paint, they add a kinesthetic mode of learning to the visual and auditory. Letter-writing activities, however, must be playful and nonthreatening. It is unrealistic and inappropriate to drill kindergarten children in correct letter formation.

Research indicates that traditional practice such as reciting the alphabet from memory does not contribute significantly to learning to read (Schickedanz, 1998). Mature readers can hear the letter *t* in isolation and know where it fits in the alphabet, what sound it makes, and how it can be combined with other letters to form words. At first, emerging readers do not have that knowledge. When children are taught alphabet letters in the context of their names and other personally significant words, they begin to see a meaningful purpose for letters and how they fit into the puzzle of creating and decoding words.

> There is substantial evidence to support a positive relationship between letter-name knowledge at the end of kindergarten and reading achievement in Grade 1 (IRA/NAEYC, 1998). But letter-naming drills in isolation or reciting the alphabet from memory do not create readers.

The problem with teaching letters in isolation, such as by reciting the alphabet, is that it separates letters from their purpose. When letters are learned one by one, children may become confused about letters' relationships to one another, as well as to the larger task of reading (Hiebert & Raphael, 1998). It is important that instruction in letter recognition and naming be embedded in meaningful print use. A balanced language arts program that provides demonstrations of the forms and functions of print, opportunities to freely explore writing, and scaffolding to the next level of proficiency will help students grow as independent readers, writers, and thinkers.

Forms and Functions of Text

An appreciation for literary forms is important to reading and writing development. When children begin to write, they tend to focus first on the functions of text—to inform, to invite, to label—but before long, they begin to attend to the different forms that text can take.

Three-year-old Haley still uses scribbles and squiggles for writing but creates a list for Santa in vertical form and a letter to Grandma in horizontal form (see Figure 6). Even though she has not yet mastered conventional letters, she has an understanding that different types of writing take different forms.

Genre is closely related to form. Kindergarten children can learn the difference between fairy tales, poems, picture books, and informational text. Understanding genre helps them make meaning from text. They learn to expect different things from "Long ago and far away" and "Dinosaurs were creatures that lived millions of years ago."

As children listen to and talk about books, they learn that stories have characters, settings, and plots. They know that some types of stories begin

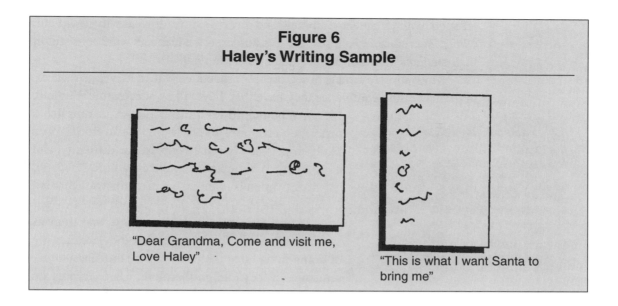

Figure 6
Haley's Writing Sample

"Dear Grandma, Come and visit me, Love Haley"

"This is what I want Santa to bring me"

"Once upon a time" and end "happily ever after." They learn words like *curious*, *fairest*, and *dragon*, which are not ordinarily part of a 5-year-old's vocabulary. Reading informational materials such as nonfiction books, catalog, and magazines to young children also contributes to their literacy development in many ways. Knowing how expository text is structured—important concepts first, details later—helps young readers understand and remember the information they read.

Of course, appreciating and understanding the elements of story are building blocks that facilitate reading comprehension and enrich language development later on (Cullinan, 1989). Through exposure to print, children develop understanding of plot structures, characters, language patterns, and other literary conventions. They notice and interpret illustrations. Even the youngest children notice patterns in literature and develop intuitive understandings about literary conventions. All are foundations for becoming effective readers. This knowledge and appreciation does not develop on its own, however. Teachers must not only generate exposure to a variety of texts, both fiction and nonfiction, but they also must provide children with an opportunity to talk to peers and adults about what they read.

Desire to Learn to Read and Write

Reading is a cyclical and cumulative learning process: The more children read, the better readers they will become; the better readers they are, the more they are likely to read. Research has shown that reading achievement is highly affected by the frequency, amount, and diversity of reading activity (Wigfield, 1997). Therefore, it is important that kindergarten teachers work to instill in their students a love of literacy and a desire to read.

Motivation to read is based on how readers view themselves as readers; in particular, the confidence they have that they will be successful (Wigfield, 1997). When children think they can accomplish a task, they are more likely to choose to do it, more likely to persist when they experience difficulty, and more likely to ultimately complete the task.

> *"Research consistently demonstrates that children need to enter first grade with good attitudes and knowledge about literacy. Otherwise they will probably find first grade instruction inaccessible."*
>
> **(Burns, Griffin, & Snow, 1999, p. 65)**

Motivation is often associated with engagement. Cambourne (1988) says that learners will be "engaged" in a task only if they perceive that there is some good reason for doing it, that they are capable of doing it, and that there will not be unpleasant consequences if they fail. Furthermore, when learners are given an opportunity to make choices and to collaborate with others, they are more likely to tackle challenging tasks.

The skills and attitudes that children acquire in kindergarten will have a significant impact on their learning in years to come. When teachers create joyful learning environments for students in which they feel confident about taking risks, are empowered to make decisions about their own learning, and have opportunities to interact with others, the stage is set for the development of lifelong readers.

For Further Reading

Ericson, L., & Juliebö, M.F. (1998). *The Phonological Awareness Handbook for Kindergarten and Primary Teachers* Newark, DE: International Reading Association. Contains lists of books, songs, and rhymes that promote phonological awareness.

Hall, D.P., & Cunningham, P. (1997). *Month-by-Month Reading and Writing for Kindergarten* Greensboro, NC: Carson-Dellosa. Provides many practical suggestions for balancing the kindergarten literacy program.

Yopp, H.K. (1995). Read-aloud book for developing phonemic awareness: An annotated bibliography. *The Reading Teacher, 48*, 538–542.

CHAPTER 4

What Does an Exemplary Kindergarten Classroom Look Like?

● ●

When the students in Mrs. Kline's kindergarten class arrive at school, they follow established routines: They sign in on the attendance sheet and then go to the classroom library corner where they browse through books until class begins.

When the bell rings, the group gathers for Circle Time at the Big Book easel where Mrs. Kline rereads a popular story. The story is an old favorite of the students, so they chime in as Mrs. Kline reads. Because they are already familiar with the story, Mrs. Kline decides to play with the words, inviting the students to correct her if she makes mistakes. The children laugh as Mrs. Kline substitutes *cat* for *bat* and *norse* for *horse*. She asks the class for help and the children join in, replacing familiar text with silly rhymes.

After Circle Time, it is Center Time, and each student places his or her name card beside a particular center name to indicate a chosen activity for the day. Some students go to the writing center to make get-well cards for a classmate who is at home with the chicken pox. Some students choose to play a number game at the computer center. A few students have appointments at the veterinarian play center, where they browse through pet brochures as they wait for the "vet" to check their stuffed animals. A few more decide to go to the building center to finish constructing a bridge they began the day before. Mrs. Kline circulates among the students, asking and answering questions and helping to guide their learning as they play.

● ●

In Mrs. Kline's classroom, play is a medium through which children learn. Throughout the day, children have opportunities to learn through play, by exploring and experimenting and by interacting with one another and with the teacher. Mrs. Kline has created a carefully planned environment that exposes students to many forms of text and tools for writing. Her goal is to implement a program that provides systematic modeling and demonstration of literacy skills in the context of meaningful reading and writing through play activities. She knows how to scaffold students to higher levels and how to intervene when additional support is needed. Most important, she understands and accepts the developmental nature of learning and creates a classroom that supports risk-taking and individual progress.

Many children experience this type of learning environment long before they enter school. They have the advantage of greater vocabularies, a stronger sense of story, more concepts about print, and richer experience banks. Sulzby, Teale, and Kamberelis (1989) maintain that "children who have had frequent opportunities to write and read emergently at home are more likely to enter conventional literacy as confident, risk-taking readers and writers" (p. 64). For this reason, Cunningham and Allington (1998) suggest that an effective kindergarten classroom is one that simulates a literacy-rich home.

Although few kindergartens can imitate the intimate, one-to-one connections that parents and children enjoy in the home, teachers must find ways to adapt these stimulating, home-like conditions to classrooms where there is 1 adult to 20 or more children, who are often from very diverse backgrounds. Additionally, the teacher must provide ways to help those children who do not have the home advantages to catch up with their peers. However, there are advantages to working with groups of children. Group activities can facilitate the development of communication and social skills, and cooperative and collaborative skills that are so important in later life.

Mrs. Kline has the advantage of strong knowledge of child development and effective literacy practices. She has access to appropriate resources for teaching young learners and an environment where learning is central, not a peripheral concern.

Learning Through Play

For kindergarten children, these important cooperative, collaborative, and cognitive skills are most effectively developed in a play-oriented environment (Owocki, 1999). Children learn from one another as they talk, listen, and play together. They learn to attend to tasks, take turns, solve problems, and express ideas. Through play, children gradually discover that other people have ideas about thinking and doing that are different from their own. This understanding has a special significance when it comes to literacy, as children must learn that not everyone, not even the teacher, will see the same meaning in their scribbled "stories."

Dramatic play also furthers literacy development. Vygotsky (1978) theorized that play enables children to use symbolic, abstract thought, which is an important precursor to reading. For example, when children begin to use one object to represent another, such as pretending a big box is a spaceship, they are developing the concept of symbolism. This can help them understand that letters represent sounds and words represent ideas. Vygotsky also emphasized the importance of a "more literate other" in the play environment; in other words, the teacher, parent, or other mature player has a key role in guiding the literacy development of children through play.

Children are active learners who constantly seek out opportunities to explore and make sense of their world. The opportunity for children in school to engage in activities of their choice helps build the skills of lifelong learning. It is important, then, for classrooms to provide an atmosphere that encourages risk-taking, a structure that provides opportunities for children to interact with one another, and an environment where children can make choices about their learning. Simply giving children an opportunity to engage in free play will not guarantee that literacy will develop. The teacher plays an important role in modeling and guiding literate behavior during play. Children are more likely to engage in literacy activities during play when teachers introduce the literacy objects such as books, writing tools, and signs, and model their use (Morrow, 1997).

Classroom Design

Careful attention to a classroom's physical design contributes to the success of a play-oriented literacy program. A classroom designed to promote optimal literacy development is full of materials to support reading, writing, and speaking. These literacy materials should be kept in clearly marked locations that are accessible to children and changed frequently to maintain their interest. The classroom should be designed to help children associate literacy with enjoyment. Partitioning the room into small spaces helps to increase verbal interaction and facilitates cooperative activity. Roskos (1995) suggests that "large open spaces encourage children to run and chase, while small, enclosed spaces invite them to converse and play quietly with one another"

(p. 9). Desks, bookshelves, plants, easels, and other large objects may be strategically placed to define boundaries.

Environmental print is print that is found in children's natural surroundings. Literacy-rich classrooms are filled with print: books, labels, signs communicating directions and other information, charts, word banks, and other displays of language abound. One of the first signs of emerging literacy in young children is recognition of print in the world around them (Miller, 1998). They see stop signs, billboards, and names of stores and fast food outlets. Because this print is personally relevant to young children, it enables them to behave like readers and see themselves as readers, which helps to build positive attitudes toward reading.

Some ways that environmental print is incorporated into the classroom are through labeling classroom objects and furniture, creating signs with directions, and displaying posters of school and community events. It is important that these labels be incorporated into meaningful literacy experiences. In order to take full advantage of print-rich environments, children must interact with the print, not just look at it. Miller (1998) points out that "unless adults draw attention to print and help children associate it with their own ideas and experiences, youngsters may not make strong connections between print and their own lives" (p. 100). In addition to drawing students' attention to existing print, teachers should involve students in creating their own signs and labels in their environment. For example, personal storage areas can be labeled "Juan's locker," "Farida's basket," or "James's hook." Even the class pet's cage, food, water, and supplies should be labeled, and may include instructions for care and feeding.

It is interesting that children generally do not recognize environmental print out of context. Often they require specific instruction to transfer familiar signs, names, and logos to conventional text (Kuby, Aldridge, & Snyder, 1994). Through consistent and repeated modeling, demonstration, and practice, the teacher can use environmental print to draw children's attention to the forms and functions of text. Mrs. Kline, for instance, will frequently change the "EXIT" sign on her classroom door to different fonts and colors to show her children that the word remains the same regardless of the style in which it is written.

Play Centers

Constructive play, which stirs imagination and facilitates language development, can be stimulated by play centers focusing on real-world contexts that are familiar to the students. Favorites include the post office, a restaurant, or a doctor's office.

It is important that these play centers also contain "literacy artifacts" that engage students in reading and writing for authentic purposes and for simple play (Neuman & Roskos, 1992). Christie (1990) reports a study in which a traditional preschool housekeeping center was flooded with print items such as recipe cards, calendars, newspaper flyers, coupons, and recipe pads. Over 4 days, 290 separate literacy interactions were observed, where previously there had been none.

In addition to dramatic play centers, the kindergarten classroom should also contain literacy centers with materials specifically designed to encourage children to read and write. A reading corner may be furnished with pillows, stuffed animals, posters, and books. A writing spot should be filled with a variety of tools and materials for writing. Literacy centers should be designed to accommodate quiet, individual learning spaces as well as a larger shared area for read-alouds, shared reading, modeled writing, and author's chair. (See Chapter 5 for a full description of classroom centers.)

The Teacher in an Exemplary Kindergarten Classroom

"Effective classroom teachers are the only absolutely essential element of an effective school." **(Allington & Cunningham, 1997, p. 81)**

The single most important element of any classroom program is a knowledgeable and effective teacher (Allington & Cunningham, 1997). In an outstanding kindergarten classroom, the teacher understands the developmental nature of learning to read and write, accepts individual differences, and adapts the instructional program to meet the needs of the students. Excellent instruction builds on what children already know and can do and develops the knowledge, skills, and attitudes necessary for lifelong learning.

In order to facilitate the literacy development of kindergarten students, the teacher must be constantly alert to opportunities to model, demonstrate, and reinforce reading and writing. In addition to planned literacy events, teachers must be always sensitive to the "teachable moment"—the serendipitous opportunity to extend learning in the classroom. Morrow's (1997) research reinforces the important role of the teacher in guiding and modeling literate behavior. She found that children are more likely to engage in literacy behaviors during play when the teacher has introduced and modeled the use of literacy materials.

The International Reading Association (2000) reminds us that excellent reading teachers

- understand child development and believe all children can learn,
- continually assess children's progress and adapt instruction,
- know and use a variety of methods to teach reading,
- use a variety of materials and texts for teaching, and
- use flexible grouping strategies to tailor instruction to individual needs.

The teacher's position in the play-oriented learning environment may range from interested observer to equal participant to expert coach.

> Teacher involvement has been found to assist 'nonplayers' to begin engaging in dramatic play, to help more proficient players enrich and extend their dramatizations, and to encourage children to incorporate literacy into their play episodes. (Christie, 1990, p. 544)

Interactions with peers are very important to learning, but the involvement of an adult who assumes the role of a more knowledgeable play partner without taking control of the play is most effective in helping young children make discoveries about the meaning of print (Vukelich, 1994).

We can see this in Mrs. Kline's classroom, not just in its organization, but in the way she deals with various students. On a given morning, she quietly observes one group in action, taking anecdotal notes that will later be transferred to student files. Then she plays along with the students in the restaurant center, "ordering" her lunch from the menu. Finally, she brings together a group of students in the writing center to give them some systematic instruction in using beginning consonant sounds. There is no question that teaching kindergarten is a complex juggling act that requires knowledge, skill, and true caring about the lives of the children in the class.

For Further Reading

Cunningham, P., & Allington, R.C. (1998). *Classrooms that Work: They Can All Read and Write*. Provides a description in Chapter 8 of what an effective kindergarten classroom looks like. New York: Addison Wesley.

Morrow, L.M. (1997). *The Literacy Center: Contexts for Reading and Writing*. York, ME: Stenhouse. Provides additional suggestions for organizing the kindergarten classroom.

CHAPTER 5

Learning Centers in the Kindergarten Classroom

Learning centers are purposefully planned classroom areas where children can work with hands-on materials to guide their own learning. If the materials and activities are well organized and the procedures and routines are carefully established, learning centers can be exciting and motivating, and can provide productive experiences that will help move students toward meaningful independent learning.

Centers provide independent, constructive learning opportunities for students. They are an excellent means of reviewing and reinforcing concepts that have been taught previously in a large-group setting. They provide opportunities for individual and collaborative use of manipulatives and materials that could not be used practically by all the children in a whole-class group. They enable the students to work with one another, to make choices both individually and cooperatively, to solve problems, and to explore their world. All of these are building blocks to independent learning.

Learning centers also offer wonderful benefits for the teacher. Materials and activities can be prepared in advance. Activities can be adapted to varying levels of skill and ability. Many different skills and learning styles can be developed and addressed. And because the teacher is not required to monitor every movement, he or she is free to work with individuals and small groups as needed.

The number and type of centers in a kindergarten classroom will vary from one class to another. Some teachers use centers as the main strategy by which curriculum objectives are achieved; some use centers for free-time choices after the whole-class lessons are finished; some change their centers according to classroom themes; and others have a set of

Why Use Learning Centers?

To provide opportunities for children to explore, discover, and create

To give teachers freedom to work with small groups and individuals

To accommodate different learning styles and intelligences

To teach independence and collaboration

To teach children to manage time, make choices, and use resources wisely

To promote teamwork and group activities

To develop both literacy and specific subject skills

34

permanent centers and change the materials and activities within them on a regular basis.

Linda Holliman (1996) offers the following guidelines for developing learning centers:

- Center activities should provide meaningful learning opportunities, not busy work.
- Center activities should be developmentally appropriate.
- Center activities should be multilevel to accommodate varying needs and abilities in the classroom.
- Center activities should provide for active learning and collaboration among students.
- Center activities should invite student choice.

Planning Learning Centers

Curriculum objectives and standards should be the foundation of the learning center plan. Ideally, learning center activities are varied and open-ended, with enough scope to provide all students with opportunities for both success and challenge, regardless of their ability levels. Think about the learning goals for the students in your classroom and plan activities and resources that will take your students from where they are to where you would like them to be. Also consider how you will evaluate your students' progress toward those goals. Assessment should be an ongoing part of any teaching-learning experience, including work in centers (see Figure 7).

The number of centers in your classroom will also depend on your instructional goals. It is a good idea to start with only a few centers, adding new ones gradually as students become familiar with the routines. Some teachers ultimately like to have as many as 12 to 15 centers in the classroom to provide students with choices while limiting the number of students who may visit each center. These centers remain in place all year, simply changing the activities and manipulatives on a regular basis, which works well for a writing center, for example. The basic structures remain constant while the tools (pens, markers, stamps, paper) are changed with themes or seasons.

Managing Learning Centers

Management is the key to effective learning centers. Basic issues such as how the materials will be stored when not in use and how the boundaries of the center will be defined must be determined before introducing centers to the class. For example, not all centers need to be on display at all times. Plastic

Figure 7
Planning Template for Learning Centers

Center Name:	Date Used:	
Curriculum Objectives:	**Method of Evaluation:**	

Learning Activities:	Materials Required:	Storage and Management System:
1.	1.	
2.	2.	
3.	3.	
4.	4.	
5.	5.	

Notes: What worked? What didn't? What changes will I make?

tubs, drawstring bags and even old backpacks may be used to store center materials. Nor do all centers require a lot of space. A placemat, tablecloth, or beach mat could be used to define the space needed for a particular center activity.

Managing movement in learning centers is also an important consideration. Many teachers offer their kindergarten students free choice of which centers to visit. Others prefer a structured approach to center movement, increasing the amount of freedom and choice as the students become more accustomed to the process and more prepared to take responsibility for their own learning. Some approaches to "managed movement" include

- rotating groups of students through centers in a prescribed order at regular intervals;

- placing students at a starting center, then allowing them to move through others as they choose;

- assigning students to the centers they must visit each day, but allowing them to choose the order in which they will visit the centers and how long they will spend in each;

- requiring students to visit one or two compulsory centers each day, but allowing them to visit others of their choice as time permits; and

- encouraging students to plan their day by "signing up" to visit the centers of their choice.

If students are given the opportunity to make choices about which centers to visit and how long to spend at them, there must be structures in place to limit the number of students at a center at any given time. Behavior problems often occur as a result of having too many children at a center. Two to four students at a center, depending on the type of activities and whether they lend themselves to partner work, seem to be optimal for kindergarten children.

There are many ways to indicate limits to the number of students in a center. For example, necklaces for each center, used to designate the number of openings for a particular center, are hung at the center or in a central location. Children choose a center by putting on the appropriate necklace. When all necklaces are gone, no one else can use that center. When a child completes her time at the center, she hangs up the necklace and looks for another center with necklaces available.

> **Management Issues to Consider**
> - Organizing and storing materials
> - Teaching students to use the center
> - Coordinating movement between centers
> - Controlling the number of students at each center
> - Teaching students how to help one another
> - Monitoring what is accomplished at centers

It is also important to have some way of tracking which centers each student visits—whether a child is returning to the same center day after day or flitting from center to center without accomplishing anything. A simple chart on which students color the centers they have visited helps them develop organizational skills and gives the teacher a quick picture of the choices they are making. As the year progresses, students may be taught to use planning forms on which they can indicate their center choices for the day or week ahead.

Until students develop the independent learning skills of monitoring their own time at a center, it may be necessary to establish a time-keeping routine. A signal may be used to indicate time to move on to another center, or students may be required to visit a certain number of centers during a set class time.

One goal of centers is to enable the teacher freedom to circulate and work with individuals or small groups. Therefore, it is important that students not come to you for assistance at every turn. One routine that must be established is for students to know how to seek help when they do not understand something. Use the maxim, "Ask three, then me," which directs students to first ask three classmates for help with a problem before approaching the teacher. Or, have children use a code such as displaying a yellow card on their table to indicate that they need assistance when the teacher becomes available. Other teachers show students a multistep process:

1. First try it yourself.

2. Then ask a classmate in your group.

3. If that person doesn't know, ask another classmate.

4. Finally, go on to something else until the teacher is available.

Like all procedures and routines, how to seek help must be taught and practiced before independence can be expected. Demonstrate for students how to decode a difficult word in a story, and then ask another student for help. Have students role-play situations to dramatize problems they might encounter in a learning center and how to ask another student for help. Teach students that they have a responsibility to help one another when asked. Clearly define the different circumstances under which you cannot be disturbed, such as when you are working with a group of students, and when you can be interupted, such as when a child becomes injured or sick. Established routines for indicating the teacher's assistance is required, such as placing a colored ticket on a table or putting a name card in a pocket chart, enables students to go on working until the teacher is free to help.

Finally, it is a good idea to monitor your students' involvement and accomplishments in the centers. Some centers will have products associated with them, such as writing, buildings, or drawings; others will be more process based. Pocket folders are very good organizational tools that students can be taught to use themselves. On one side of the folder, students can keep their planning form or record sheet; on the other side, they can store papers or projects completed in the centers. If carrying a folder from place to place seems cumbersome for your kindergarten students, have them keep materials in personal baskets or cubbies. Plastic ice cream containers work well for storing individual student materials. Systematic observations and anecdotal records maintained by the teacher will round out the record-keeping component of center use.

Teachers must decide what system works best for them and their students, keeping in mind the learning goals of the students and level of independence at which students are capable of functioning, and always being prepared to make changes that accommodate the needs of the students.

Teaching Routines and Procedures

As mentioned earlier in this chapter, if centers are to be meaningful learning experiences, the routines and procedures must be modeled, taught, and reinforced before students can be expected to participate independently. When learning centers are not successful, it is often because time has not been taken to teach and practice the procedures. As with any new learning activity, center routines first must be discussed and demonstrated by the teacher. Then students need ample opportunities for guided practice and reinforcement before they can be expected to work independently.

It is a good idea to teach one center at a time. Model and demonstrate the activities and manipulatives in the center, then provide the students with opportunities to explore them with guidance. Allow those students who can work on their own to visit the center first. Gradually allow others to join the center as they demonstrate ability to work independently. Observe the center until you are confident that students are using the area productively before introducing a new activity.

Although the teacher is responsible for designing learning activities and monitoring students' progress, there are many ways that volunteers and paraprofessionals may contribute to the learning center classroom. Volunteers might be responsible for setting up centers and keeping track of materials. They might model the use of artifacts in the center and stimulate student involvement by playing along with them. Having volunteers circulate among the students to provide assistance and monitor behavior helps learning centers run smoothly.

> Some teachers hold "Center School" to teach students the routines and procedures of learning centers. It is important to remember that any new learning experience requires opportunities for modeling and demonstration, guided practice and feedback, and independent application.

Only when you feel confident that your students are capable of accomplishing the tasks independently should you move on to teaching another center. Establishing the necessary routines for learning activities, record keeping, movement between centers, and seeking help may take several weeks, but it is worthwhile. Taking time to teach will ensure that your students gain the most benefit and motivation from the centers.

Common Types of Centers in the Kindergarten Classroom

There are three main types of centers commonly found in kindergarten classrooms: literacy centers, discovery or exploration centers, and dramatic play centers. The literacy center is generally the focal point of the classroom and contains both reading and writing components. Discovery or exploration centers enable students to explore materials with a core curriculum focus, such as science, the alphabet, or art. In addition to specific literacy centers, it is important that all centers have a literacy component and contain a variety of print materials appropriate to the center's theme. Dramatic play centers usually focus on simulations of real-life experiences for students, such as housekeeping, shopping at the supermarket, or visiting the hospital.

The Literacy Center

The literacy center is likely to be the focal point of your classroom, with quiet spots for reading and writing, as well as a gathering place for discussions, read-alouds, modeled writing, and other large-group activities. The reading corner and the writing spot are the two main elements of this center and should be available to students from the first day of school.

The Reading Corner: The reading corner is usually a favorite place in the classroom. Make it inviting and comfortable with soft cushions, stuffed animals to cuddle, and stacks of wonderful books. Scour garage sales for an old upholstered chair or sofa, purchase or sew beanbag chairs and oversized pillows, and ask for carpet remnants at flooring stores. If possible, place the reading corner near a window where there will be plenty of light. Use a cardboard appliance box for a book nook, or enlist the assistance of a talented volunteer to build a reading loft.

> A classroom library should contain 8 to 10 books per child, with about 25 new books circulated each month, as well as old favorites that are maintained all year.

Morrow (1997) recommends that the classroom library contain 8 to 10 books per child. Although regular visits to the school and public libraries are important, research has shown that children who have access to books in the classroom read up to 50% more than students in classrooms without libraries (Bissett, 1970, in Morrow, 1997). Be sure to provide a variety of types of books, from picture books to poetry, informational books to magazines, store catalogs to brochures. After reading a book aloud, place it in the reading corner for students to visit again. Big Books and class-made books are particularly popular items.

A study by Hickman (1979, in Martinez & Teale, 1987) found that emergent readers are more likely to try to read books that are predictable and familiar to them. Books should include simple vocabulary, stories told entirely by pictures, and a selection of illustrated children's storybooks. While about one third of the books should be changed each month, old favorites may be kept on display longer, even for the entire year.

It is essential that books in the kindergarten classroom library be stored within easy reach of students. Whenever possible, display books with front covers, rather than the spines, facing out. Literacy artifacts add appeal to the reading corner and encourage further interaction with books: A Franklin-the-Turtle doll, Lily's purple plastic purse, or a Rainbow Fish puppet invite dramatic play around books. These artifacts, puppets, and props assist in story retellings and role dramas. A listening post with inexpensive portable tape recorders may be used to listen to stories on audio tapes, which are available commercially or can be created by the teacher. Students in upper grades might be asked to record story tapes, or parent volunteers may be willing to make recordings complete with sound effects.

> *"A broad experience with a variety of stories, informational books, and poetry is fundamental to children's continuing growth in reading and writing."*
> **(Martinez & Teale, 1988, p. 571)**

It is never too early to begin fostering reading for enjoyment. There is much evidence that the best predictor of and a causal factor in children's growth in reading and vocabulary is the amount of leisure time spent reading (Fielding, Wilson, & Anderson, 1986, in Martinez & Teale, 1987). A carefully planned and inviting reading corner helps children experience the joy of reading from their earliest days in school.

The Writing Spot: The writing spot is the other integral component of the literacy center. It should be filled with a variety of paper sizes and tools for writing, which are changed on a regular basis. The use of unlined paper is important for emergent writers. Researchers have found that lined paper limits the opportunity of young children to construct their own ideas about writing and drawing and placement on a page (Sulzby, Teale, & Kamberelis, 1989). Other writing spot materials should include staplers, scissors, tape, glue, date stamps, and butterfly clips. Any teacher who has found more staples than words on a piece of writing can verify the importance of teaching students how to use this equipment purposefully. (See Figure 8 for tips for designing the writing spot.)

Writing letters and notes to others will be the most personally significant writing children will do, and nothing is more exciting for them than receiving a message from someone else. A system of mailboxes (made very simply

Figure 8
Tips for Designing the Writing Spot

- Use heavy cardboard folders or old boxes to create private offices.
- Place real desks in pairs to make the writing spot a special place to work.
- Search garage sales for an old desk with lots of nooks and cubbies for storage.
- Provide a special author's chair to encourage children to share their writing. Include a working typewriter or computer and a microphone for author's chair.
- Post a photocopied list of all the names of students in the class, along with their pictures, so students can write notes to one another.
- Include students' birthdays and old greeting cards for the students to cut, paste, and recycle.
- Provide writing tools of all sorts—markers, crayons, pencils, chalk, pens, and stamps. Change and add to these items frequently to maintain motivation.
- Keep a bulletin board available to display student writing.
- Establish a mailbox system or message board for students to write notes to one another.
- Pair with a higher grade class to answer letters to Santa or to the class pet.
- Provide a variety of sizes, colors, and types of paper on which to write, preferably unlined— recycled newsletters or worksheets work fine. Adding machine tapes encourage students to write l-o-n-g stories!
- Use dry-erase boards, minichalkboards, and magnetic writing boards to encourage children to write letters, words, and stories.
- Provide staplers, scissors, tape, and glue for book making; date stamps for use on every piece of writing; and key rings, clothespins, or oversized paperclips for attaching cards and papers.
- Provide rubber stamps or stickers for children to write rebus stories.
- Encourage children to write about their injuries in "The Ouch Book." Provide a bound book for children to write in, along with a list of various body parts for them to copy—as well as band-aids to put on the appropriate illustration.

by attaching empty milk cartons together) or a message board can facilitate this process. You may also want to post a photocopied list of all the students' names in the class, along with their pictures, to help everyone get their letters to the appropriate recipients.

In addition to the group gathering place, there should be spaces for quiet, independent work or pair sharing. Kindergarten children are usually accustomed to working at tables, so "real" desks borrowed from another classroom make writing an especially "grown-up" activity. Personal workspaces also may be created from heavy cardboard or old boxes.

A special place for an author's chair encourages kindergarten children to share their writing. A microphone is exciting for young children to use and helps ensure that others can hear what the author is saying. When invited to read what they have written, regardless of the form of the writing, children view themselves as writers. They also begin to develop a sensitivity to the distinctions between oral and written language (Martinez & Teale, 1987).

Do not wait until midyear to introduce the writing spot. Writing should be an expected daily activity for students from the first day of kindergarten (see Chapter 10).

Discovery and Exploration Centers

Discovery and exploration centers are learning centers that invite children to explore and manipulate artifacts, make discoveries, and solve problems related to a subject or theme. All exploration centers should include books, signs, opportunities for writing, and other literacy activities:

- A math center may include stamps and stickers for creating story problems, contests in which the students must write estimates and guesses, and books such as *The Doorbell Rang* by Pat Hutchins.
- An art center may include signs to label and title pictures, and books with distinctive art styles, such as Barbara Reid's plasticine illustrations in *The New Baby Calf*, or Eric Carle's collage-style illustrations in *The Very Hungry Caterpillar* or *The Grouchy Ladybug*.
- A multicultural center may have cards with the names of countries to match with those on a map or globe, and a graffiti wall along with the book *Talking Walls* by Margy Burns Knight.
- A science center with a geology theme may have informational picture books with which to compare rocks, and books such as *Everybody Needs a Rock* by Byrd Baylor, which encourage oral language development as children share their ideas about how to choose the perfect rock.
- A seasonal center may include books such as *The Jacket I Wear in the Snow* by Shirley Neitzel, along with pictures of clothing to sort and label. The book and clothing could be rotated as the seasons change.
- A theme center may include books such as *The Ocean Alphabet* by Jerry Palotta for an ocean theme and objects and pictures to sort by initial consonant. Change the theme, books, and objects periodically to maintain student interest.

Dramatic Play Centers

Dramatic play centers simulate real-life situations that encourage children to learn through interactive play. Whether the center is a store, an office, or a kitchen, it is important to include objects and artifacts that encourage and develop literacy skills (see Figure 9).

Figure 9
Literacy Artifacts for Dramatic Play Centers

Center	Traditional Objects and Artifacts	Objects to Enhance Literacy Development
Carpentry Center	Hardhat and goggles, toolkit, workbench (with carpeting underneath to reduce noise), plastic connecting pipes, pegboard, labeled containers of nails and screws, wood blocks, hammer, and screwdriver	Blueprints and plans, trade magazines, signs ("Caution," "Kids at Work," etc.), materials for creating plans and signs Suggested books: Anything by David Macauley
Grocery Store Center	Shopping baskets and small carts, food packages and play foods, cash register and play money, and grocery bags	Coupons, advertisements, checkbooks, posters, credit cards, shopping cards, and paper for making signs and ads
Kitchen Center	Measuring cups and spoons, food packages, dishes, telephone, toy appliances, sink, towel, play food, and table and chairs	Recipe books and cards, food coupons and advertisements, catalogs, telephone book, and message board (refrigerator magnets)
Pet Store or Vet's Office	Stuffed animals, dishes, grooming materials, cleaning materials, and play medicine	Brochures on pet care, information to sign in for appointments, labels, and clipboard
Restaurant	Tables, dishes, cutlery, and play food	Menus, notepads for taking orders, signs with "specials"
Hospital	Bed, blankets, bandages, dolls, pill bottles, rubber gloves, stethoscope, toy thermometer, and toy syringe	Signs, clipboards, hospital bracelet, admission cards, and prescription forms

In conclusion, management and organization are keys to effective learning centers. Fountas and Pinnell (1996) remind us that "every moment invested in teaching routines is time well spent, because it will save hours of instructional time later" (p. 62). It is important not only to teach students how to complete the learning activities but also how to conduct themselves while in the center, how to take care of and store the materials, and how to make the transitions from one center to another. Any inappropriate behavior can be minimized by establishing clear expectations and teaching routines, but it may be necessary to establish consequences such as withdrawing from center activities any student who disregards procedures. Frequent misbehavior, however, may be a sign that the center activities are too difficult or the management procedures are unclear or unsuccessful.

Organizing the class around learning centers teaches more than literacy:

> You are helping children understand how to conduct themselves as members of cooperative groups. They are learning how to fulfill commitments, manage time, manage tasks without constant reminders and supervision, conserve materials, collaborate with others, and respect others' rights. (Fountas & Pinnell, 1996, p. 65)

When students learn to organize and monitor their own learning, they are well on their way to becoming independent learners.

For Further Reading

Saskatchewan Education. (1994). [Online]. Available: http://www.sasked.gov.sk.ca/docs/ kindergarten [2001, August 7]. Contains excellent information on designing, organizing, and managing literacy centers in kindergarten classrooms.

PART II

Strategies for an Effective Kindergarten Classroom

Interactive Storybook Reading: Making the Classroom Read-Aloud Program a Meaningful Learning Experience

The storybook read-aloud has long been an integral component of the kindergarten literacy program. Reading to children is a vital way to encourage the development of concepts about print, story structure, and other elements of text. During story time, children learn that a book is read from front to back and that there is a difference between pictures and print. They hear new and interesting words and begin to make connections between letters and sounds. They enjoy vicarious experiences not possible in real life. They also find out that things can be learned from books and that stories can be enjoyed again and again. Story reading, perhaps more than any other activity, provides the child with a wealth of information about the processes and functions of written language. Storybook reading is a powerful element in the development of young children because it provides language instruction in a meaningful holistic context, not sequenced and isolated as subskills (Strickland & Taylor, 1989). The benefits of story reading include

> *"Reading to children is the single most important activity for building the knowledge required for eventual success in learning to read."*
> **(Hoffman, Roser, & Battle, 1993, p. 496)**

- building vocabulary;
- developing an understanding of story structure;
- enriching experience banks;
- helping to make the connection between letters and sounds;
- reinforcing concepts about print;
- encouraging higher level thinking;
- teaching reading processes in a meaningful context;
- modeling fluent, expressive reading; and
- motivating an interest in reading and books.

But even the venerable practice of reading aloud has been the subject of controversy in recent literature (Teale & Yakota, 2000). Too often, the storybook read-aloud has been an "add-on" to the classroom program, with only cursory attention paid to the selection of books and the teaching opportunities it provides.

Although story reading is a pleasurable activity in itself, simply immersing children in books will not turn them into readers. Teale and Yokota (2000) caution that reading aloud is not a "silver bullet" (p. 14); the selection of materials and the way they are read will determine the effectiveness of the read-aloud program in nurturing children's literacy development. Three keys to an effective classroom read-aloud program are

- selecting high-quality literature that extends children's knowledge of literature, language, and the world;

- active participation by children that constructs knowledge and extends thinking; and

- rereading familiar text to reinforce children's knowledge of the reading process and how words go together.

Selecting Books for a Read-Aloud Program

Given the quantity of excellent children's books published today, the most difficult task for the teacher is to make selections. With so many books to choose from, it would be foolish to waste read-aloud opportunities on literature of marginal quality. Galda and Cullinan (2000) advise teachers to "choose books that capture your students' interests...and stretch them as readers" (p. 137); therefore, it is important for teachers to be readers themselves, and to keep current in the ever-expanding world of children's literature.

> *"All children need to find themselves and meet new people in the stories they read."* (Galda & Cullinan, 2000, p. 142)

When choosing storybooks for young children, look for themes to which children can relate. Familiar situations with an unusual twist enable readers to connect existing knowledge with new ideas. Characters in books for young readers should be clearly defined and few in number, preferably containing one main character with whom children can identify. Young readers prefer children or animal characters that think, act, and talk like children. The plot should be fast-moving and logically sequenced, with a realistic problem and a satisfying conclusion. The author's theme or message should be subtle but appropriate to the world of a 5-year-old. Choose text that extends children's range of vocabulary and sentence fluency, and illustrations that not only enhance the text, but tell a story in themselves.

Children need to see their own lives reflected in the books they read. As our school populations become increasingly diverse, we need to ensure that all children are represented in classroom read-aloud selections. When we read stories from a diversity of cultures, we honor all students in the class, and we teach them to appreciate both the differences and the similarities of all those around us. In selecting multicultural literature, look for books that are accurate, authentic, and that avoid stereotypes of a culture in either text or illustrations.

Although most books read to kindergarten children will be picture books, be sure to include a variety of genres such as biography, poetry, and fantasy. It is also important to expose young children to a balance of fiction and nonfiction texts. There are many beautifully crafted informational books for young children on a variety of topics to match almost any classroom theme.

Nonfiction books for kindergarten read-alouds should be up-to-date and factually accurate; avoid a combination of fact with fiction or opinion, and be sure the books have pictures that accurately portray the action, mood, and intent.

How to Read Aloud

Most of us do not spend a lot of time planning the read-aloud program. After all, there is no wrong way to read aloud, is there? There are ways, however, to make the classroom read-aloud program a more effective learning experience. Careful selection of books that extend children's vocabulary and background experiences is a first step. But it is through purposeful teaching that we also extend students' thinking and their knowledge of the reading process.

Effective storybook reading is an interactive process. Too often, we fail to give children the opportunity to interact with text while it is being read, insisting that they wait until after the reading is done. Sipe (1998) found that children's responses to story read-alouds that had the greatest quality and quantity of discussion actually occurred *during* rather than *after* the reading. Based on these findings, Sipe suggests that allowing children to talk during the

Elements of Effective Read-Aloud Books for Kindergarten

- Simple, well-developed, action-oriented plot that the children can relate to, preferably with an element of surprise at the end
- Lots of dialogue
- Familiar situations that may incorporate new, unusual, or different events
- A simple and satisfying climax
- One main character with whom the children can identify
- A variety of ethnic, cultural, and racial backgrounds that are authentic and do not reflect stereotyping
- Themes that represent suitable values
- Illustrations that support and enhance the text
- Language that is rich and melodic and extends the vocabulary of the students

story reading "may offer the possibility of scaffolding the children's meaning construction as it is in the process of being constructed" (p. 378).

If we wait until after reading to discuss a story, we are missing out on valuable literacy opportunities. When the teacher precedes the reading by inviting predictions and personal connections, she is creating a context for the reading. Taking time to discuss and clarify difficult concepts during the reading can prevent misunderstanding further on, and encouraging students to respond during the reading enhances both comprehension and interest in the story. Pausing to confirm and revise predictions, ask questions, and make inferences lays the groundwork for independent reading. Children learn that understanding text is a process that occurs before, during, and after reading.

Before Reading

Before reading aloud, it's a good idea to preview the book and practice reading it with fluency and expression. Plan an introduction that will provide a context for the reading. A good way to do this is to find links to the children's personal experiences. Introduce the title, author, and illustrator. Children may be interested in other elements of the book such as a dedication or publication date.

Introduce any information that may be necessary to facilitate understanding of the story. For a fiction reading, this may include something about the main character, setting, genre, point of view, or author's theme. This step is particularly important when the reading is a nonfiction text, to find out what the children already know about the topic and ensuring that they have enough background knowledge and vocabulary to understand the text.

Set goals or purposes for listening to the story. "I wonder" statements, such as "I wonder what the wolf wants to do with the pigs," provide a focus for listening. Predictions invite higher level thinking and develop reading strategies. You may want to flip through the book and discuss the pictures (called a picture walk) to make predictions.

> When selecting culturally diverse read-aloud materials, look for books that
>
> • avoid stereotypes (negative or positive),
>
> • reflect the cultural group authentically,
>
> • use natural language,
>
> • validate the experiences of children from that culture, and
>
> • broaden our vision and invite reflection.
>
> (Adapted from Galda & Cullinan, 2000)

During Reading

Read fluently and expressively, varying your tone, volume, and pitch as you read. Hold the book so that the children can see the illustrations. Try to establish frequent eye contact with the students. Draw their attention to illustrations and features of text. (This is particularly important for nonfiction text.) Point out charts, diagrams, and organizational aids.

As you read, model your own responses to the story. Pause occasionally to revisit predictions that you and the students have made, to express curiosity or confusion, or to comment on something you found interesting. Invite the students to question and comment as well, but keep the discussion focused on the story.

Be sure to explain ideas or words you think the students might not understand. Feel free to improvise if you feel a concept needs elaboration or replace a word that you feel is inappropriate. Interaction with the students throughout the reading will help to ensure that they understand the text as it is read.

Ten Teachers' Choices for Kindergarten Read-Alouds

Miss Bindergarten Gets Ready for Kindergarten (Joseph Slate)

Strawberry Mouse and the Big Hungry Bear (Audrey Wood)

Jillian Jiggs (Phoebe Gilman)

The Mitten (Jan Brett)

The Very Hungry Caterpillar (Eric Carle)

Red Is Best (Kathy Stinson)

Thomas's Snowsuit (Robert Munsch)

The Wide-Mouthed Frog (Keith Faulkner)

The Kissing Hand (Audrey Penn)

Happy Birthday Moon (Frank Asch)

Jesse Bear, What Will You Wear (Nancy White Carlson)

After Reading

After reading, be sure to allow time for discussion. Encourage various levels of response, such as "What did you like?" and "What would you have done if you were the character?" Sometimes you will want to ask questions to extend students' thinking about the text and sometimes you will want their unprompted responses. One teacher has found that if he simply pauses after the reading, the students will start talking about the story. A key comprehension strategy for readers of all ages is to make personal connections to the text. A prompt such as "What did this story remind you of?" can help students relate the reading to their own experiences or other stories they have read.

Retelling: The retelling strategy is an effective tool for assessing and enhancing comprehension (Gambrell & Dromsky, 2000). It requires children to think about story structure, distinguish main ideas, and use the language of the story. However, before kindergarten children can retell a story effectively, they must be provided with frequent and consistent instruction (Gambrell & Dromsky, 2000). Model retelling of stories, clearly defining the beginning, middle, and end, as well as such information as the characters' names and important events. As children become familiar with the process, invite them to join you in a retelling. Start the story and invite children to add to it. Provide scaffolded practice by prompting students if they falter or get off track, and by prompting students as they retell. When retelling a story, teach students to tell

- who the main characters are,
- where and when the story took place,
- what important event or problem started the story,
- what important things happened in the story, and
- how the story ended.

Extension activities: Sometimes after-reading activities are necessary, but some stories lend themselves to these activities more readily than others. Extension activities should develop naturally from the text and extend students' literacy development and higher level thinking. Some effective extension activities include

- rereading the same text,
- reading another text by the same author or about the same topic,
- dramatizing the story or parts of the story,
- adapting the story into a class-made book or informational report,
- responding through art and crafts,
- responding through writing, and
- extending through related events (such as cooking, field trips, or guest speakers).

Sometimes talking about the book is all the follow-up that is needed; often the best follow-up to reading is rereading. Always make the books available to students after a read-aloud. Research has shown that these are the books children are most likely to choose for independent reading (Martinez & Teale, 1988). It is important that repeated readings be part of all components of the reading program. There is great value in rereading a book a second, third, and even fourth time (IRA/NAEYC, 1998). A good story will present new insights to be gained from each reading. Rereading familiar texts also enables us to revisit the text to focus on the mechanics of letter-sound relationships, language patterns, and sentence structures. It helps reinforce language development and familiarizes students with genre and story structure, which appears to be particularly important for children at risk (Morrow, O'Connor, & Smith,1990). And, of course, be sure to put the read-aloud book in the classroom library, as the children will want to peruse it again and again.

Reading aloud is an important way to develop skilled and willing readers. It gives teachers an opportunity to expose children to vocabulary and concepts they would not be able to read on their own. They learn about the language of books and the structure of story. By explaining words and ideas as needed, you provide students with access to new and complex concepts, creating background knowledge on which to build further learning. And through sensitive guidance of children's questions and discussion of the story, you are able to bridge even the youngest students to higher levels of thinking and responding.

CHAPTER 7

Shared Reading: Learning to Read by Reading

When parents read to children at home, it is a happy and secure experience in their lives. The physical closeness and bonding that occurs while reading a book, combined with the pleasure of a mutually satisfying activity, creates a positive association with books that can a last a child all his life.

It seems that some children learn to read almost magically, just by being read to. Yet Durkin's (1966) classic research shows that most children who came to school reading had been the beneficiaries of much incidental instruction from parents. When parents and children share in reading a book, they usually talk about the pictures and text, and recite familiar passages together. They point out letters and identify words. These interactions with text create a solid foundation for learning to read.

In an effort to simulate the "bedtime story" event in a school setting, Holdaway and colleagues (1979) in New Zealand created the "shared book experience." By enlarging the text of stories to make it visible to groups of children, they were able to model the reading process and draw children's attention to concepts about print and letter knowledge that they would not otherwise gain from simply listening to a story read aloud. This was a wonderful classroom strategy because it not only enabled groups of children to participate in the reading of a book, it also accommodated a variety of developmental levels. Each child could gain different things from the same lesson. For example, during one shared book experience, some children could learn basic concepts about print, such as reading left to right and top to bottom, while others could make connections between letters and sounds and still others could learn elements of literary language.

Features of the Shared Reading Strategy

- **The text is enlarged so that all readers can see it.**

- **Lessons are fast paced and interactive.**

- **A single shared-reading experience can address varying developmental levels of students.**

- **The text is read aloud several times, with students invited to join in.**

- **Concepts about print and reading strategies are explored using the shared text.**

Classroom Strategies for Shared Reading

During a shared reading lesson, students participate and observe as the teacher uses a song, poem, chart, or Big Book to demonstrate the use of reading strategies. The teacher may choose to think aloud as she reads, explicitly teaching students a process for decoding, questioning, or self-correction. On subsequent readings, the teacher may use the opportunity to draw students' attention to graphophonic features such as initial consonants, or conventions of print such as exclamation points. The text is read several times, with students reading chorally with the teacher as they become comfortable and familiar with the text. The shared reading lesson is designed to be fast-paced, interactive, and multilevel.

Although any text may be used for shared reading, rhymes, songs, and predictable stories are most popular. Text with features such as rhythm, rhyme, and repetition are appealing to children and motivate them to participate in the reading. Different genres and formats—such as Big Books, overhead transparencies, language experience charts, pocket charts, and interactive charts—may be used for a variety of different purposes.

Teacher Choices for Shared Book Experiences in Kindergarten

Brown Bear, Brown Bear, What Do You See? (Bill Martin Jr)

Is Your Mama a Llama? (Deborah Guarino)

Over in the Meadow (Olive A. Wadsworth)

Cookie's Week (Cindy Ward)

Rosie's Walk (Pat Hutchins)

The Jacket I Wear in the Snow (Shirley Neitzel)

How to Conduct a Shared Book Experience Using a Big Book

Big Books are trade books printed in enlarged format. Shared reading of Big Books enables the teacher to model and demonstrate reading strategies using full-length stories. There are many commercially produced Big Books, but teachers can create Big Books with their students. When choosing commercial Big Books for shared reading in kindergarten, choose books with simple, repetitive language and illustrations that closely match the text. Large print, with only one or two lines per page, supports beginning reading. (See Chapter 6 for before-, during-, and after-reading experiences, pages 52–55.)

There are many materials that can be used to highlight text in a Big Book or on a chart without making permanent marks. Wikki Stix, or waxed yarn, can be stuck on the pages. Removable highlight tape comes in a variety of sizes and colors. Reading wands, which can be as simple as a chopstick with nail polish on the end, may be used to track lines of text or point out individual words. Word frames may be commercially purchased or made by cutting a box shape in the center of a small file card.

Take a look into a kindergarten classrom at a shared book experience in action:

● ●

Boys and girls, now that we have finished reading *The Jacket I Wear in the Snow,* go back and look for this word (Hold up word card *the*). Can anyone read this word? Can you find this word on the word wall from last week? Let's call out the letters—T-H-E. Would someone lead us in a word cheer? [Give me a T! T! Give me an H! H! Give me an E! E! What have you got? THE!] Can anyone come up and point out the word *the* on the first page of the book? [Use pointer or wand. Use a word framing card to isolate *the* from the text around it. Review the letters, t-h-e.] Do you notice that there's a space before the *t* and after the *e*? That tells us that it is a separate word. Let's highlight this word *the* by putting a circle around it with Wikki Stix. Can anyone find another *the*? Oh, do you notice that the *T* on that word *the* is different from the *t* on the other word? That's called a 'capital T,' and we put it on the first word in the line. In the air, let's all make a capital *T*. A straight line down and a line across the top. Now let's make a lower case *t*. Straight line down and a line across part way, but not all the way to the top. [Invite students to highlight all the *the* words they can find on the page and count them.] Now, in Center Time, you might want to get this book, or another book, and see how many *the* words you can highlight.

● ●

Shared Reading Using Overhead Transparencies

Any form of text such as poems, songs, or stories can be reproduced on an overhead transparency. Words, phrases, graphophonic elements, punctuation, and other elements of language can be noted using overhead markers or highlighting tape. An overhead projector placed on the floor to project onto the wall can make a wonderful literacy center for a small group of students.

Shared Reading Using Language Experience Charts

Language experience charts enable children to see their talk written down. The children generate ideas that the teacher transcribes, explaining what she is doing as she writes. (Chapter 9 gives a detailed description of language experience as a shared writing activity.) Experience charts are a wonderful medium for shared reading activities, as it is particularly meaningful for young children to read their own words in print.

One type of language experience activity is to invite each child to contribute a line to a prompt such as, "I liked the ___ at the museum," or "I am thankful for ___." Each child's line may be added to the experience chart for all to see:

- Jeffrey is thankful for his grampa.
- Sara is thankful for her striped socks.
- Maria is thankful for her baby brother.
- Truong is thankful for his new book.

Take advantage of this authentic reading experience to revisit the chart many times. Because this writing is connected to objects or events in their lives, emergent readers will have an easier time reading it and will often copy from it when writing independently. The experience chart is also a resource for reinforcing the following concepts about print:

- Can you find your own name?
- Can you find a word that begins the same as *David*?
- Can you find a word that has "twin" letters?
- Can you find the letter *p*?
- Can you find a word that you know?

You may want to assemble the chart into a class Big Book. Cut the chart into individual lines and give each child his own line. (Some children may be given the opportunity to cut their lines into individual words, then reassemble them like a jigsaw puzzle.) The children can glue their lines to large pieces of paper and add illustrations. These pages may be laminated and coil bound for durability into a class Big Book, which is guaranteed to be a popular item in the classroom library.

> **Add actual photographs of students to their pages. One teacher made a class book using the pattern from *It Looked Like Spilled Milk* by Charles G. Shaw. She took a picture of each child looking up and pointing at the sky, then the children glued their own photos to the page, along with their cut-out cloud pictures.**

Shared Reading Using Pocket Chart Stories

The pocket chart is a particularly useful literacy tool for drawing children's attention to lines, phrases, and words in text, and reinforcing the important concept that words are separate entities with spaces around them. Lines of text, often poems or nursery rhymes, are written on strips of paper and placed in the clear plastic pockets for students to read and manipulate. Although there are many ways to use this text, it is most effective for students to move from whole text to component parts—line-phrase-word—then back to the whole text.

Johnson and Louis (1987) suggest that the following sequence of shared language activities using pocket charts is appropriate, first for whole lines, then phrases, and finally words:

> Draw students' attention to lines, phrases, and words by framing; that is, cupping your hands around the beginning and end of the featured text. This is more effective than pointing, because it defines the beginning and end of the chunk of text.

Recognizing text: After reading the whole text several times, draw attention to individual lines. Read each line, framing it as you read, then ask, "What does this line say?" Invite students to respond, then have the whole class "read" the line together.

Identifying text: Read the text, framing each line as you read, then ask, "Where does it say…?" The children must respond by framing the appropriate line.

Matching text: Prepare a second set of sentence strips for the pocket chart text. Display the complete rhyme in the pocket chart or tacked to the wall. Beside it, arrange the second set of sentence strips in a mixed order. Ask students to read the first line and find the sentence strip that matches it. When a strip is identified, hold it directly under the other line for students to determine whether it matches. If there is an incorrect match, ask a student to explain why it is does not match.

Sorting text: When students are thoroughly familiar with the text, put the strips in the pocket chart in the wrong order and have students sequence them. This activity may not be appropriate for all kindergarten students, but it would be a useful challenge for those who are beginning to read. Remember the responsibility to extend the learning of every child, including those with advanced skills.

The activities of recognizing, identifying, matching, and sorting text may then be extended to other chunks of text. After working with whole lines, focus on meaningful phrases, then individual words. Allow the children to see you cutting up the sentences to reinforce the concept of individual words. Keep tools such as a pair of scissors, markers, highlighting tape, and some extra sentence strips tucked into the pocket chart at all times.

Modified cloze activities (Johnson & Louis, 1987) involve removing from the pocket chart individual words one or two at a time for students to identify. Turn the word card backward, cover it with a sticky note, or replace it with a blank card as a word marker. When the missing word is guessed, return it to its place. Start by removing only a few words, and each time the routine is repeated, remove more cards. When working with words, always start with concrete nouns first, then action verbs, and finally modifiers. "Structure words" such as prepositions, pronouns, articles, and auxiliary verbs are the most difficult to identify in isolation.

Some variations of modified cloze include

- having the missing word cards displayed for students to find and replace;

- giving the word cards to individual students as they are removed, and as the text is read, each child replaces "his" word as appropriate; and

- removing all but structure words, and have the children rebuild the rhyme, word by word, and reread the rhyme frequently as it is built.

Substitution routines are other activities that beginning readers enjoy. Reading a rhyme with substituted words or a story that does not make sense has great appeal for the 5-year-old sense of humor. Display the full text of the rhyme or story. Beside it, display a sentence strip with one word substituted in the line. (For example, *Jack and Jill went up the street.*) Read the incorrect line aloud and invite children to

- identify the incorrect word,

- name the correct word,

- frame the word that must be substituted, and

- find or print a card with the correct word.

Shared Reading Using Interactive Charts

Interactive charts enable children to physically manipulate elements of text. Manipulable elements of text may include entire lines, phrases, or individual words such as rhymes, names, concrete nouns, number words, or active verbs. Interactive charts are created by preparing a rhyme, song, or finger play in enlarged text, and providing a means by which certain chunks of text may be removed or replaced by another. (See Figure 10 for a sample activity.) For example, in the nursery rhyme, "Jack be nimble, Jack be quick, Jack jump over the candlestick," the name can be changed each time, such as "Kyle be nimble, Kyle be quick."

In a song like "Old McDonald Had a Farm," children may substitute different animals and their corresponding sounds. This can lead to many opportunities for developing phonological awareness, such as counting syllables, rhyming words, or matching initial sounds.

Figure 10
Sample Interactive Chart Activity

Write on sentence strips the words to the rhyme:

"Popcorn, Popcorn, Yum, yum, yum,
Don't you wish that you had some?"

Glue the strips to a large chart or board. Use sentence strips with contrasting colors on the background paper to help students see where the lines begin and end.

Read or sing the text (depending on the text and your talent), tracking each word with your finger or a pointer. Take time to reread and enjoy the text many times as a whole before drawing attention to specific text elements. Do not introduce a manipulation until children are totally familiar with the text as a whole. On another day, revisit the text to introduce the interactive component. Have some replacement words, such as *pizza*, *cookies*, or *chocolate* already prepared. Substitute the new words and read the rhyme together each time. Invite individual students to track the words as they are read.

Invite students to offer ideas for replacement words. Write their suggestions on word cards and read the text with the new ideas in place. Clap out syllables in words: pop-corn; rice; pep-per-o-ni; cha-pa-ti.

Have the chart and manipulatives available for students to work with during independent reading or center time.

There are several ways that a chart can be adapted to facilitate manipulation:

- Attach paper fasteners to the chart, so that word cards can be hole punched and allowed to hang in place.

- Use a small piece of Velcro, magnetic tape, or sticky tack on both the chart and the word cards.

- Create a transparent pocket using a piece of acetate taped over the word(s) to be substituted.

Participating in shared reading activities can make a powerful impact on children's literacy development. Dickenson (1989) found that a shared reading program "dramatically increased children's engagement with books and print in particular" (p. 229), helping them construct knowledge about print and develop self-confidence as readers. However, he cautioned that the type of text, pace of lessons, and focus on textual features inherent in a shared reading experience usually creates limited opportunities for extended dialogue about the story and does little to develop higher level thinking (Dickenson & Smith, 1994). Therefore, it is important that the shared book experience be just one part of an overall balanced literacy program that provides many opportunities for reading by, with, and to students, in order to nurture all aspects of their literacy development.

For Further Reading

Johnson, T., & Louis, D. (1987). *Literacy Through Literature*. Richmond, ON: Scholastic. Provides a detailed description of shared reading experiences using sentence strips in the pocket chart.

Schlosser, K., & Phillips, V. (1992). *Building Literacy with Interactive Charts*. New York: Scholastic. Suggests many good ideas on using interactive charts.

CHAPTER 8

Independent Reading by Children

It is never too early to begin to foster recreational reading habits. There is substantial evidence that the amount of leisure time spent reading is an excellent predictor of and a causal factor in children's growth in reading and vocabulary (Fielding et al., 1986, in Martinez & Teale, 1987). In fact, research by Lapp, Flood, and Roser (2000) indicates that, not only do kindergarten and first-grade children who read more score higher on literacy assessments, they also perform better on measures of general knowledge.

> "A broad experience with a variety of stories, informational books, and poetry is fundamental to children's continuing growth in reading and writing."
>
> (Martinez & Teale, 1987, p. 571)

The more accessible books are to children, the more likely they are to read. Books should be placed all around the classroom, within easy reach of students. The books in the classroom library should represent a variety of genres:

- Poetry
- Informational books
- Big Books
- Class and student-made books
- Picture books
- Biographies
- Multicultural stories and folk tales
- Magazines, newspapers, and brochures

It may be too much to expect kindergarten children to focus on one book for an extended period of time. Hickman (1979, in Martinez & Teale, 1987) found that the most common activities among kindergarten and first-grade students during independent reading time were browsing and flipping through books, rather than concentrating on one story. It is also unrealistic to expect silence during independent reading time in kindergarten. Most children prefer to connect with others as they interact with books, and even those who read alone are likely to verbalize aloud as they read. In fact, Forester and Reinhard (1989) admit that "once it was acknowledged that Uninterrupted Sustained Silent Reading was neither silent nor uninterrupted, and consisted of little actual reading, we simply called it book time" (p. 56).

Kindergarten children do engage with books in a variety of ways. Sulzby (1985) notes that children go through a set of predictable stages in their ability to acquire stories from books. Long before they can actually decode the words, children who have a rich literacy background are able to "pretend read," turning pages of a book and telling the story, using the words and expressions of "book language." Sulzby identifies the following stages in storybook retelling:

> **Take time to teach children to engage independently with books. Model and demonstrate the different ways to read a book in kindergarten to acknowledge the various stages at which children will be functioning:**
>
> **1. Look at the pictures.**
>
> **2. Make up a story by reading the pictures.**
>
> **3. Read the words that you know.**

- At the least mature level, the child simply labels or responds to the pictures on each page, with no evidence of connected story.

- At the next level, the child actually creates his own story, using the pictures in the book and his own background experience.

- Eventually, a transition is made between oral and written language, in which the child creates a story that is influenced by the text in the book. It may include patterns or even phrases from the actual text.

- By this time, the child may refuse to try to read at all, because he has begun to understand enough about the reading process to know that he is not able to read all of the words conventionally.

- Finally, the child begins to make sense of the print, using a variety of strategies to decode words and comprehend text.

What Kind of Books Do Kindergarten Children Read?

Choice is a key to engaging kindergarten children in reading (Lapp et al., 2000). When children have a variety of books accessible to them, they are more likely to spend time interacting with books. They enjoy revisiting books that have been read aloud or used for shared reading. In fact, Martinez and Teale (1988) found that when children selected classroom Big Books, they were more likely to try to read conventionally.

Although independent reading is not considered to be a learning objective for all children in kindergarten, many children will begin to read conventionally before the end of the school year. There are differing opinions on what types of text most effectively support emergent reading (Teale & Yokoto, 2000), but three types of texts are most commonly used in early childhood classrooms today: predictable stories, decodable text, and literary text. There are advantages and disadvantages to each.

Predictable Stories

Predictable stories, such as Bill Martin Jr's *Brown Bear, Brown Bear*, enable all children to experience success in reading by relying on pictures, repetition, and predictability to access the text. Because of the nature of the text, the vocabulary is usually quite simplistic and the story line limited. Although this type of reading engages students and builds their confidence in reading, it does not provide them with word-solving strategies and contributes little to their sense of story or reasoning skills.

Decodable Text

Decodable text refers to books in which most or all of the vocabulary is phonetically regular. Often, in an effort to maintain phonetic consistency (*Nan can fan Dan*), the language may be unnatural and the story line nonexistent. Some children find safety in the phonetic predictability, but others are unmotivated by the stilted text. Children may be unwilling to read these books, and if they do read them, the contrived syntax prevents children from using any word-solving strategy other than decoding. In fact, some of the books are actually more difficult to decode because of the irregularity of some short vowel sounds (*All the cats sang to the stars*).

Literary Text

Literary text has the advantage of interesting story lines, beautiful illustrations, and rich language, but because no effort is made to control vocabulary or syntax, these books often are too difficult for emerging readers to access independently.

It is evident that a combination of these three types of texts provides the balance most early readers need. Publishers are recognizing this need and are generating increasing numbers of "little books" (8 to 24 pages) that tell a story using a combination of decodable and high-frequency words, attractive illustrations, and concepts that are accessible and appealing to young children.

Leveling Texts

The practice of leveling texts, developed by Marie Clay (1991) to help teachers provide reading materials of graduated difficulty for students in Reading Recovery, has gained increasing popularity in classrooms (Fountas & Pinnell, 1996; Weaver, 2000). Based on the knowledge that instructional-level text is optimal for reading instruction, most teachers are striving to instruct all students using texts with just the right balance of challenge and support (see Figure 11).

It is important that kindergarten children have access to a variety of resources and opportunities for learning that meet their developmental needs. Popular wisdom suggests that many children are not ready for formal reading instruction in kindergarten (Saskatchewan Education, 1994). However, we as teachers must be ready for those who are, and provide the opportunities and resources each child needs to take him from where he is to where he can be.

Figure 11
What Leveled Texts Look Like

For Emerging Readers	For Developing Readers	For Fluent Readers
Enlarged text and spaces between words, placed consistently on each page.	Enlarged text, may be integrated with illustrations or on different places on the page.	May be entire pages of text without illustrations.
Highly predictable and patterned language—from single words to one or two sentences.	Language is natural but choppy; almost entirely high frequency and decodable words.	Language is more flowing; increasing literary language.
Illustrations closely match the text.	Illustrations support but do not match text.	Illustrations enhance the story, not the text.
Realistic events and concepts that children can relate to.	Several sentences on a page but line breaks are in meaningful chunks.	Increased numbers of characters and dialogue.
	Beginnings of a story line, twist at the end, mostly realistic.	Stories more imaginative and less likely to be in reader's realm of experience.

(L.J. Rog & W. Burton, 2001)

Choices for Independent Reading Time

There are many alternatives that enable children to enjoy and benefit from independent reading experiences, including Reading Around the Room, sharing reading materials, early reading books, author or theme centers, and audiotaped books.

Reading Around the Room is an activity in which children simply travel around the room reading all the print they can find. Provide a variety of pointers to track each word as it is read and make sure that classroom environmental print is displayed at the students' eye level. Keep a basket of tools on hand to be used as pointers for tracking words—wooden chopsticks, rulers, flashlights, batons, even back scratchers. Try the discount stores at Halloween for such pointer items as slip-on "witch fingers," "magic wands," and "shark sticks" that move their jaws.

Shared Reading Materials

Remember that students love to read materials that previously have been read in class. Make poetry and experience charts available for student reading. Laminate the charts for durability, which will enable children to use washable markers on them. (Use clothes hangers with clips to store oversized charts.) Attach sentence strips from pocket charts together with a metal ring, and have them available as "puzzle poems" for children to put back together.

Early Reading Books

Keep a collection of beginner books on hand for students who are ready to "really read." Store them in three or four plastic baskets, color coded with stickers on the books, to help children choose books at different levels of difficulty. Students quickly learn that if they can read one yellow-sticker book, they will be able to read another from the same basket.

Author or Theme Center

Books should be part of every classroom learning center, regardless of the theme, but you also may want to have specific literacy centers that focus on an author such as Eric Carle, or a literary theme such as alphabet books. Store special theme books in an old suitcase or other special container and teach students to return the books to their places.

Audiotaped Books

Listening to a story on tape while following along in the book is a wonderful way to combine reading aloud, shared reading, and independent reading.

Many excellent books on audiotape are available commercially. If you make your own, be sure to include a signal to remind the reader to turn the page. If your classroom has a listening post with headphones, you will want to establish clear procedures for determining who selects the book, who operates the cassette player, and so on. An inexpensive alternative is individual, portable cassette players with earphones.

Classroom Routines and Procedures

As with all classroom activities, it is necessary to establish routines and clarify expectations for children during independent reading time, which should include the following routines and procedures:

- How to take care of books
- Returning books to their proper place after reading
- Maintaining appropriate voice volume during quiet reading
- Getting a new book without disturbing others
- Finding places to read
- Knowing signals for beginning and end of reading time

Teaching any routine takes time and patience. Allow plenty of time for modeling, demonstration, and guided practice before expecting students to function independently.

There is probably no better model for a love of reading than a teacher who integrates reading and writing into every aspect of the classroom program. A take-home reading program that extends the reading experience beyond the classroom helps children to see literacy as part of their lives as well. There are few classroom activities that are so simple, yet so powerful in nurturing children's literacy development.

For Further Reading

Fountas, I., & Pinnell, G.S. (1996) *Guided Reading: Good First Teaching for All Children.* Portsmouth, NH: Heinemann. A good resource for additional texts for beginning readers.

CHAPTER 9

Writing *For* and *With* Children: Modeled, Shared, and Interactive Writing

Modeling is the most powerful tool in a teacher's instructional toolbox. Modeling writing for students not only demonstrates how writers think and work but also validates this process. Modeling writing shows it is an important and meaningful activity that grownups do, in life as well as in school.

Modeling and demonstrating the mechanics and processes of writing involves students at a variety of levels (see Figure 12):

Modeled writing is "writing out loud." The teacher demonstrates for students the processes involved in putting ideas down on paper and vocalizing thoughts while writing. The students are merely observers.

Shared writing involves students in generating ideas for writing, but the teacher is the scribe, talking through the process while recording students' ideas.

Interactive writing takes the process one step further by allowing students to share the pen with the teacher. They collaboratively record ideas on paper, with the teacher scaffolding the student who is writing and demonstrating for the remainder of the students who are watching.

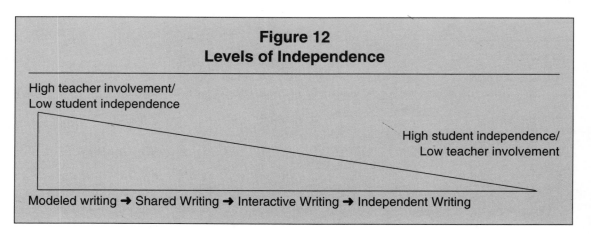

Figure 12
Levels of Independence

High teacher involvement/
Low student independence

High student independence/
Low teacher involvement

Modeled writing ➜ Shared Writing ➜ Interactive Writing ➜ Independent Writing

A Modeled Writing Experience: The Morning Message

In a modeled writing experience, the teacher explains that good writers write by talking about ideas and then organizing them in their heads. The teacher describes the mechanics of writing, such as putting spaces between words, inserting capitals and periods, and "stretching" words to hear all the sounds. The teacher also shows how to add to or change an existing piece of writing. In this process, the students are observers, not participants.

Modeled writing may be used to teach minilessons about process, conventions, or style, such as

- how to decide what to write about;
- different forms of writing—a letter, a poem, a report, an invitation;
- beginning and ending a sentence;
- "stretching out" a word to hear all of its sounds;
- using punctuation;
- choosing the best word; and
- editing and making changes.

The morning message is one example of modeled writing in action. It usually takes the form of a welcome and preview of the events of the day. Not only is it a useful literacy tool, it also establishes routines and helps children organize the day.

The teacher may say as students write,

> **The modeled writing lesson is a particularly good opportunity to draw children's attention to sight words such as *the*, *are*, or *when*. These are structure words that "glue" writing together, but are often difficult because they are not decodable and carry little meaning in themselves.**

• •

Boys and girls, today is Tuesday, January 12, so I'm going to write that right off the bat. T-t-t —*Today* starts with *t*. I make it a capital *T* because *Today* is the very first word in my sentence. *To-day* has two parts. Now I'm going to leave a space after *Today* because that's the end of that word, and the next word is *is*. I'm sure that word's on our Word Wall. Sure enough, there it is up there— *Is* —i-s. *Tuesday* is the name of the day, so I'm going to put a capital *T*, and *January* is the name of the month, so I'm going to put a capital *J*. January. Let's clap that word together and count the parts: 1-2-3-4. What do I want to say next? Well, I want to say that the firemen are coming to visit today. That's what I'm going to say: *The–firemen–are–coming–today*. Five words.

• •

Because the morning message is created each day by the teacher, it can include specific words, language patterns, and concepts that need to be taught to the class. Also, it enables the teacher to include language that meets the needs of all the students in the class. As with any whole-class activity, it is important that the morning message include both successes and challenges for all students, regardless of their abilities.

Shared Writing Through Language Experience Charts

Shared writing has its roots in the language experience approach, a strategy developed by Sylvia Ashton-Warner (1983, in Button, Johnson, & Furgerson, 1996) in which the teacher transcribes texts dictated by the children and uses these texts for instruction. Traditionally, language experience activities were designed mainly for documenting children's language and experiences. Today, shared writing is used for the additional purpose of enabling children to see the processes that a skilled writer uses. However, the language experience activity may still be used to generate student ideas for shared writing.

Language experience charts enable children to see their talk written down. As children contribute ideas, the teacher writes them down, modeling and demonstrating the process of writing. Experience charts may be used for daily news time, recount of a field trip, a collaborative report on a topic, statements about the "person of the day," and retelling or response to a story.

A powerful use of language experience activities is to elicit a response to a book or a prompt from each student in the class.

Teachers may want to model writing a few students' responses, but it is neither interesting nor educational for students to sit through the transcription of every student response in the class. Therefore, keep the shared writing activity brief—about 10 minutes at most—then gather the rest of the students' comments individually or in small groups.

The learning from this activity can be extended by writing all students' responses on a large chart. Revisit the chart the next day for students to "read" their own responses, and take advantage of this chart as a medium for shared reading.

When completed, the individual pages may be bound into a class book for the classroom library or take-home reading program. These class-made books are favorite choices in

The following books provide springboards for children to generate their own ideas for language experience:

Things I Like by Anthony Browne

Miss Bindergarten Gets Ready for Kindergarten by Joseph Slate

The Important Book by Margaret Wise Brown

the reading corner. Another alternative for a class book is to wordprocess the students' comments in an enlarged font.

An Interactive Writing Activity

McCarrier, Pinnell, and Fountas (2000) describe interactive writing as "a dynamic literacy event in which reading and writing come together" (p. 67). In an interactive writing lesson, the teacher and students share both the composing and the writing. Heavily scaffolded by the teacher, students from the group are invited to "share the pen" to write parts of the message. The remaining students learn from the modeling and dialogue.

Together the students and teacher create a message. The teacher selects individual students to write parts of the message, based on her knowledge of each students' knowledge and capabilities. For some students, it may mean writing the first letter of their name; for others it may mean being able to write some sight words or letter patterns. Here is an example of an interactive writing activity:

● ●

Teacher: Boys and girls, we're going to write a letter to thank Mr. Jones for driving us in the schoolbus to the museum. If this is a letter, how do you think it should start?

Student: Dear Mr. Jones?

Teacher: Good suggestion! Letters almost always start with Dear Somebody. So, we need to write that word *Dear*. Let's listen for the beginning sound: d–d–d. David, that's the first letter in your name; would you like to come up and write a capital *D* for us? Boys and girls, do you see how David makes a straight line down and a fat round tummy on the D? The word *Dear* is not anybody's name, but we make it a capital *D* because it's the first word in the sentence. The rest of the word is *ear*. Let's stretch out the word together: D–ear. Watch while I write the middle letters *e–a*. Can you hear what sound is at the back door of *dear*. Who can write a lowercase *r* at the end? Carmen, that letter is in your name, can you write it for us?

After the word *Dear*, we have *Mr. Jones*. We have to leave a space between *Dear* and *Mr.* because they're two separate words. William, would you please come and put your hand here as a spacer so we remember to leave a space between the two words?

Now, the word *Mr.* starts with *mmm*. Corey, I bet you know how to write the word *Mr.* Tell me out loud. Would you like to come up and write it on the chart?

William, come up and be our spacer again. Jessica, becausse *Jones* is your last name, would you please write it after the space? Boys and girls, do you notice how Jessica puts a capital *J* on *Jones* because it's the first letter in a name? Can we say the letters Jessica just wrote? J–o–n–e–s. And now, after that word *Jones*, I'm going to put this little squiggle, which we call a comma. Let's say that word together—*comma*. We always put a comma after Dear Somebody. Now, let's read that part together: Dear Mr. Jones.

• •

This lesson is probably long enough for one day. The next day you might collaborate on a sentence of thanks, followed by a closing to the letter. These daily writing projects can be very short and can be continued over several days in order to maintain student interest. It is a good lesson for them to see one writing activity extend over a few days.

In the 10-minute interactive writing exercise, nine concepts about language and print were demonstrated:

1. Letters start with "Dear Somebody."
2. The first word in a sentence starts with a capital letter.
3. Names start with capital letters.
4. Words can be stretched out to hear beginning and ending sounds.
5. Words have spaces between them.
6. *Dear* starts with the same sound as *David*.
7. Capital *D* is made with a straight line and a round tummy.
8. A comma comes after the greeting in a letter.
9. Print says the same thing every time you read it.

Shared and interactive writing enable beginning writers to go beyond what they can do independently. They learn words and how they go together. They learn letters and how they are connected to sounds. As beginning writers generate ideas and participate in the process of conveying these ideas in standard form, their learning is scaffolded to higher levels of understanding of how ideas are conveyed in letters, words, and sentences, and then built back up to meaning again. "Through interactive writing, language and literacy comes together" (McCarrier, Pinnell, & Fountas, 2000, p. 237).

For Further Reading

McCarrier, A., Pinnell, G.S., & Fountas, I. (2000). *Interactive Writing: How Language and Literacy Come Together, K–2.* Portsmouth, NH: Heinemann. A good source for more information on writing with children.

CHAPTER 10

Writing by Children

Kindergarten children should be expected to write every day. Daily writing helps develop an understanding of the forms and functions of print. As they experiment with letters and other symbols, children construct knowledge about letter-sound patterns. Partridge (1991) found that students who participated in daily writing scored significantly higher in spelling ability than those who wrote only once a week.

Martinez and Teale (1987) noted that when they did not initiate a writing program until several weeks into the school year, many children refused to participate, saying that they did not know how to write. But when writing was introduced on the first day of school, not one student objected to participating. "Instead they seemed to accept the request to write as simply one more strange event in a day full of strange experiences" (p. 445).

> **From the first day of kindergarten, children should be expected to write every day.**

Stages of Writing Development

Our first writing goal at the kindergarten level is to encourage children to put down their ideas on paper (see Figure 13). This written communication may take a variety of forms, ranging from picture stories to "scribble writing" to actual alphabet symbols. Children in kindergarten will be at many different stages in their ability to communicate their ideas in writing. Through experiences with print and opportunities to write, children discover that there is a connection between the letters they write and the sounds in words.

When students start to represent the sounds they hear with letters, they are demonstrating a key understanding of the phonetic principle of language. At first, they may represent entire words with a single initial consonant. Then they usually add final consonants, such as *bk* for book or *tp* for top. Later, medial consonants are added, then finally long vowels and short vowels. Short

---

Figure 13
Tips for Encouraging Writing in Kindergarten

Demonstrate and reinforce how to hold a pencil *before* bad habits emerge.

Model and teach young writers to say what they are writing as they write it, so they do not lose track of their thoughts.

Insist that children attempt to write a word before getting help with conventional spelling. When providing assistance, work with what they know.

> For example, if a child is adamant that he wants the conventional spelling of the word *computer* and he has spelled it *cmpudr*, point out that he has five out of the eight letters correct and show him where he has omitted or used incorrect letters.

Recognize that writing is a social activity. Allow students to work with partners. Encourage them to ask classmates for help.

Train students to date stamp and put their names on all writing.

Model, demonstrate, reinforce, remind, and rehearse appropriate attitudes and behaviors.

Provide lots of opportunities for sharing *before*, *during*, and *after* writing.

Develop an effective storage system to keep copies of students' writing as a record of oral and written language development over the course of a year.

Analyze students' work from the beginning to find out what they are capable of and what they need to be taught.

---

vowel sounds are the most difficult for young readers to hear and to spell correctly. It is essential that children be encouraged in their approximations of letter formation and spelling. This is the way that they construct knowledge of how our language goes together, and ultimately become confident and competent writers. One way to encourage and honor developmental stages in spelling is to model different ways to write in kindergarten:

- Sometimes you just make squiggles or scribbles.

- Sometimes you draw pictures or symbols.

- Sometimes you write the letters that you know.

- Sometimes you write the letter you hear at the beginning of the word.

- Sometimes you s-t-r-e-t-c-h out a word to write as many sounds as you can hear.

- Sometimes you know what a word looks like in book writing.

- Sometimes you can copy the words from somewhere in the room.

Because children will be at different stages of development in writing, it is important to legitimize the writing they are doing, while providing structures to scaffold them to the next level. Some teachers say children's writing is "magic writing" because they are at the stage in writing where they know the functions of print but are not yet aware of sound-symbol relationships. You may tell children they are "magicians" because they are the only ones with the magic power to read their writing, which is distinguished from "book writing," which anyone can read.

Isolated drill and practice in letter formation or copying conventional writing is not considered to be developmentally appropriate in kindergarten (Saskatchewan Education, 1994). Instruction in specific skills of letter formation and spelling is most effective when it is presented in the context of authentic reading and writing experiences (Reutzel, Oda, & Moore, 1989). Teacher modeling helps children see how the letters should look. There are many play-based activities in which children can practice letter formation, including tracing letters in sand, finger paint, and even chocolate pudding. Insisting on correct letter formation at this point may inhibit children's ideas. However, through carefully structured experiences with print, children learn that using letters makes the writing readable to others.

Writing Workshop in Kindergarten

Writing workshop or writing time provides opportunities for children to write independently on topics of their choice. Begin with a read-aloud, shared reading, or modeled writing activity to generate interest in writing and to demonstrate a specific learning objective. However, children will not always need a stimulus for writing. In fact, the more frequently they write, the less difficulty they have thinking of topics to write about. Often the various tools and artifacts in the writing center will be motivation enough to start children writing.

While students are still gathered together after a demonstration, ask them to explain what they intend to write about. Children have many things to think about when they write—how to form letters, how to represent sounds, or how to put ideas together. If they can verbalize ideas before writing, it taxes their working memories less when it comes time to write. As each child relates his idea, he may be given a blank sheet of paper or a writing scrapbook to begin writing. The verbalizing process also enables children who struggle for ideas to hear what others are going to write. And it allows those who have ideas to get started. An effective prompt for kindergarten writing is "Tell me what you know about...."

As children write, the teacher should circulate around the room, offering encouragement, assistance, and scaffolding as needed. Whenever possible, an adult should be available at a writing center to provide support and encouragement to the young writers.

At the end of writing time, or when it appears that the children are ready to move on, call the students together to listen and share. This is an ideal time to incorporate Author's Chair so that students can share their writing with the group, which encourages the routine of courteous listening and positive response.

This writing workshop routine establishes a number of themes for the kindergarten classroom:

- Everyone will write every day.
- Everyone writes in different ways.
- Everyone has to think of topics to write about.
- Everyone will have a chance to share his or her writing.
- Everyone will receive compliments and praise for his or her writing.

Sharing Writing With Others

Sharing writing with others is a key element in the kindergarten writing program. Students share before writing by discussing the topic and planning what they are going to write; they share during writing as they explore written language, problem solve the spelling of words, and talk about their writing; and they share after writing when they sit in the Author's Chair to read their completed writing.

The most powerful motivation for writing is the knowledge that someone else will read it. Through modeled, shared, and interactive writing of letters and messages, children learn that you can ask questions, get information, and extend friendships with others. Support children in the creation of messages and letters to others by posting a list of their classmates' names in the writing center and establishing a mailbox system.

Author's Chair

An elegant Author's Chair can be created simply and inexpensively by decorating a resin lawn chair with ribbons and glitter glue. You may even want to involve the children in the decorating. An inexpensive microphone helps to amplify tiny voices and adds to the appeal of the Author's Chair.

The Author's Chair is a wonderful way to encourage kindergarten children to share and listen to one another's writing. When the audience is taught to listen and respond politely, young writers get the message that their writing has value. Of course, these behaviors must be modeled and reinforced:

Five-year-old Matthew has just finished scribbling a story about clowns in the circus, when his teacher asks him if he would like to read his story aloud. "I can't read," says Matthew sadly. Matthew's friend Trevor, who has been listening to the conversation, jumps in. "I can't either. But you just have to sit on that magic chair—and poof!—you can read!" Then he proves his point by sitting on the Author's Chair and reading his own scribbles to the class: "'I like to watch the lions at the circus....' See? It works!"

• •

Responding to Writing

Teach the students to always respond positively to the author's work. (The time for constructive criticism will come in later grades.) Talk about what compliments are and model appropriate comments:

> Your story was funny when the dog licked your face.
>
> What an interesting word you used—"crinkly."
>
> I didn't know that frogs had stripes. I learned that from your report.

Not only does this type of modeling provide specific and positive response to writing, it also teaches the other students what makes writing good.

There are also certain behaviors expected of the writer. For instance, the writer must know what he or she is going to say—not necessarily a given for children who are not aware yet that print carries a consistent message. The writer must read in a voice that can be heard. If a microphone is not available, teach children to speak loudly and clearly.

Supporting Children's Writing

Martinez and Teale (1987) recommend that, whenever possible, there should be an adult available at the writing center, to help children who are struggling to get started, to provide encouragement for work in progress, or to facilitate sharing of completed work. Unlike other centers in the classroom, the writing center involves activity for which many children will need support if they are to learn and grow as writers. This support person may be a volunteer or a paraprofessional; it does not need to be the teacher, although the teacher will want to visit the writing center regularly to monitor student progress. Each child's needs will be different in the writing center, and even the briefest

Figure 14
How to Help Children at Different Levels of Maturity

If children are...	Then encourage them to...
still just drawing pictures,	tell about their drawing and use whatever writing symbols they know.
using a combination of random letters, symbols, and pictures,	add details to the drawing and tell about it and to separate the writing from the drawing.
writing strings of letters,	tell what is happening in the story and to make letter-sound connections.
demonstrating left to right directionality and using letter-to-word correspondences (2 for *to* or b for *boy*),	listen for beginning and ending sounds and to make spaces between words.
using beginning and ending sounds and separating words,	add vowels, and to copy words from around the room.
using invented spelling and some conventionally spelled words,	write longer pieces and begin to edit.

contacts with a skilled writer can move a child who is blocked or encourage the child who lacks confidence. Bouas, Thompson, and Farlow (1997) describe these brief contacts as "honeybee conferences" in which the adult "alights" for a short time to provide instruction and encouragement: "Honoring children's attempts to communicate by putting something on paper is the first order of business in each honeybee conference" (p. 8).

As you circulate among the children in the writing center, ask them frequently to "tell what you wrote." This encourages children to view themselves as writers, reinforces the connection between written and oral language, and develops the concept that print carries a constant message. (See Figure 14 for ways to encourage children's writing, depending on their levels of maturity.)

To Transcribe or Not to Transcribe?

Teachers differ in their attitudes to and practice of transcribing children's emergent writing to conventional print. Some teachers like to have a record of the intent of the writing. Others believe that this undermines beginning writing and forces the understanding that print carries a consistent message. It is important for teachers to consider carefully their purpose in any learning activities and to adjust their practice accordingly. Occasionally, for assessment and record keeping or for public display, it might be useful to tell children that you are going to print their story in book writing as well as their own writing. Most of the time, however, emergent writing may be left to stand alone as children use it to construct their knowledge of how print is used to convey ideas.

Teale and Yokota (2000) remind us that even 15 years ago, writing in kindergarten was virtually unheard of. Today we realize that when we invite children to write in their own ways, we honor their developmental stages and lay the groundwork for effective communication of ideas. Independent writing provides opportunities for kindergarten children to practice what they know about writing and experiment with writing conventions. And just as important, it tells children that their ideas have enough value to be preserved in written form and read by others. Few literacy experiences are more powerful than that.

For Further Reading

Freeman, M. (2000). *Teaching the Youngest Writers: A Practical Guide*. Gainesville, FL: Maupin House. Provides many practical suggestions for writing workshop in kindergarten and first grade.

CHAPTER 11

Playing With Language

In recent years, there has been intense dialogue in what has been called "The Great Debate" about phonics and whole language, a debate that has become as much political as pedagogical. In spite of the media attention, most practitioners and researchers agree that effective balanced literacy instruction includes systematic word study taught in the context of authentic reading and writing experiences (IRA, 1997). There is general consensus that the understanding that words are made up of sounds (phonological awareness) and that written letters correspond to spoken sounds (phonics) are key concepts for beginning readers. However, if phonics instruction is to be truly effective in developing independent readers, it must be embedded in a total reading-language arts program (IRA, 1997).

> *"Sharing the excitement, fun and beauty of our language can become a natural part of every day."*
>
> **(Furr, 1996, p. 7)**

Concepts about print and elements of language are constantly reinforced in all aspects of the balanced literacy program. When children listen to stories read aloud, they expand their vocabularies and hear the sounds in words. When children participate in shared reading and writing activities, they learn to match oral language to print. As they take up the pen in interactive or independent writing, they construct knowledge about how letters go together to make words and sentences and stories.

Integrating Language Play Into Read-Aloud Time

During read-aloud time, the teacher can draw children's attention to the words in the title of the book and comment on interesting or descriptive words throughout the reading. After children become familiar with a book, it can be revisited to note aspects of language. Rhyming books and alphabet books are among the best resources for language play. Alphabet books reinforce initial consonant sounds and build vocabulary. Children learn to connect familiar

82

objects and pictures to alphabet letters and sounds. In the kindergarten favorite *Miss Bindergarten Gets Ready for Kindergarten* by Joseph Slate, there is a student's name for each letter of the alphabet. Other popular alphabet books for kindergarten include

Eating the Alphabet by Lois Ehlert

The Wildlife ABC: A Nature Alphabet by Jan Thornhill

From Acorn to Zoo by Satoshi Hitomura

It Begins with A by Stephanie Calmensont and Marisabina Russo

The Icky Bug Alphabet Book by Jerry Pallota

Dr. Seuss's ABCs by Dr. Seuss

Books with rhyming text also have great appeal for kindergarten students, and draw their attention to the rhythms of language. The beginning reading books by Dr. Seuss have been extending children's reading development for five decades. The ridiculous rhymes and rollicking rhythms have great appeal for readers of all ages:

There's a Wocket in My Pocket

One Fish, Two Fish, Red Fish, Blue Fish

Mr. Brown Can Moo, Can You?

Hop on Pop

Green Eggs and Ham

Songs like "Willoughby Walloby, Woo," "Down by the Bay," and "I Like to Eat Apples and Bananas" build phonological awareness and other language skills by involving students in manipulating words and sounds.

Children also enjoy alterations of familiar tales and fractured fairy tales, but they must know the original story thoroughly in order to appreciate the new version. Read an old favorite aloud, occasionally substituting a silly word for the original to help hone listening skills and story sense—but be prepared for laughter at such comic delights as "Once upon a time there was a little boy named Little Red Riding Hood," or "Jack sold the cow for a handful of broccoli." Marilyn Tollhurst's *Somebody and the Three Blairs* is a favorite fractured fairy tale for kindergarten children.

Integrating Language Play Into Shared Reading Time

Language concepts are an integral aspect of the shared reading experience. Always read the poem, chart, or story several times for meaning and sound before isolating phrases, words, and letters. When students are familiar with the story, invite them to participate in activities focusing on language. Because the concept of "word" is a critical understanding at early stages of literacy development, every opportunity should be taken to reinforce it. Use word frames and pointers to track words one at a time as you read. Provide masks and frames to isolate words. Invite students to highlight words using markers, highlighting tape, or waxy yarn.

The following are language elements that might be addressed in shared reading lessons:

- Where to start reading (concepts about print)
- Words have spaces around them (concept of 'word')
- Rhyming words or word families (rimes)
- Specific letters and sounds, blends or digraphs
- "Words we know" (high frequency words)
- Punctuation marks

Show What You Know

Show What You Know is based on a strategy described by Richgels, Poremba, and McGee (1996). It simply involves inviting individual children to point out any features of language that they notice in a piece of shared text. Some children may point out familiar letters or letter combinations; others may recognize actual words. Punctuation marks, capitals, and other features of text may be noted.

At first, the teacher models the process, highlighting a particular feature of text, such as "a capital R, like in my name." Then students are invited to come forward individually to "show what they know." The strength of this strategy is that it enables each student to interact with the text at his own level, honoring the knowledge that he brings to the activity, and facilitating him as he extends his learning.

Other Language Play Activities

There are a number of ways to have fun with language:

- Have students clap or tap the syllables in the words as they read, to reinforce the awareness of the sounds in words.
- Reproduce portions of text on sentence strips for students to put back in order.

- Use a cardboard mask with a sliding window to cover a certain word in the text. Encourage students to predict the word, then confirm or change their predictions as you uncover one letter at a time.
- Write individual words on word cards for students to match with words in the whole text.
- Invite students to look for specific letters or patterns (for instance, "twin letters," or "st" combinations).
- Have students select key words to substitute for those in the text. Write new words on sticky notes over the old words and read the revised text together.

Integrating Language Play Into Writing Experiences

Modeled writing provides an excellent opportunity to stress letter-sound relationships, phonetic patterns, and unique spellings of words. As teachers model the transcription of oral language into print, they are constantly modeling listening for sounds and representing those sounds on paper. Teachers also should model strategies for accessing words in environmental print to use in writing:

> I can find that word *love* right up on our Word Wall. If I want to write a happy birthday note to Andrew, I can find his name right here on the class chart.

Create alliterative sentences or tongue twisters using modeled, shared, or interactive writing. Tongue twisters reinforce awareness of letters and sounds. The key is not to "twist the tongue," but to reinforce letters and sounds. Write a sentence using as many words as possible with the same sound and invite children to read with you. Ask students to suggest other words with the same sound. They also will enjoy helping to create tongue twisters.

Silly rhymes are other writing activities that focus on sound patterns. Students also may help compose silly rhymes (the sillier the better) using words that are on the word wall, in other environmental print, or in a shared or read-aloud experience.

> What rhymes with *like*? Spike...hike...bike.... Can you make a silly rhyme with any of these words? I'd like to take a hike with a spike.

When children begin using conventional letters in their own writing, encourage them to stretch out words to hear all the sounds and try to represent each sound they hear with a letter or letter combination. This is a good time to draw attention to correct letter formation, as children begin to use them in their writing.

Systematic Language Study

All these experiences are integral to effective literacy instruction. However, many kindergarten children still need experiences that systematically draw attention to the features of print, particularly the alphabetic principle.

> Stretching out words is an excellent way to develop phonemic awareness and apply it to writing. Tell children to think about the word as a big elastic band. Using their hands, they may even pretend to stretch the word as they segment its sounds, and then "spring" it back to normal as they say the word.

Instruction in specific skills such as letter recognition and letter-sound correspondence is most effective when presented in the context of authentic reading and writing experiences. Reutzel, Oda, and Moore (1989) found that teacher-led lessons in concepts about print significantly improved students' understanding of print concepts but had little effect on overall reading ability. In other words, instruction in isolated skills improves those skills, but does not necessarily improve reading. In fact, Reutzel and colleagues found that simple immersion in print had a more significant effect on reading readiness and word reading abilities than did the isolated instruction in concepts about print.

Learning Language Concepts Through Names

The most important word for any child is, of course, his or her own name. For most children, their names are the first words they learn to write. Even children who do not have the background experiences or fine motor skills to print their own names can often recognize them in print. Marie Clay (1975) reported that letter recognition and letter-sound correspondences are most effectively reinforced in the context of words that are important to a child, such as his own name. McGee and Richgels (1989) agreed that teaching letter names and other concepts about print using children's names taps into the egocentric nature of young children, honors their existing literacy knowledge, and provides a meaningful context for developing an understanding of conventions. (See Figure 15 for activities using name words.)

Hall and Cunningham (1997) suggest that teachers create a name or word wall to teach and reinforce language concepts through children's names. The letters of the alphabet are posted on a wall, with space under each for adding names and other words. Each day, a different student's name is featured and posted on the word wall. Even an unused chalkboard can be used for a word wall. One teacher used a metal chalkboard and attached the words using magnetic tape. This made the words easy to remove and replace for use in interactive writing and other language activities.

The advantages of a name wall for word study are numerous. Learning about letters, sounds, and other concepts about print is presented in the context of words that are significant to the children. It is more effective than the traditional "letter of the week," which presents the letters in isolation (Hiebert & Raphael, 1998). Although independent readers can study the letter *t* and know how it fits into the alphabet, beginning readers do not have that ability. Even singing the "Alphabet Song" may be meaningless memory work, as evidenced by Big Bird's musical rendition of the word "Abbacadefgahijuk ulimnoquerstuvuwexyazee" on Sesame Street.

The name wall also can be used as a reference point for other word study. As you draw students' attention to words, point out that, "This word starts the same as *Dylan*," or "This word ends like *Sunil*." When all the students' names have been posted on the wall, start to add other words that are important to them, such as *I*, *love*, *my*, *mom*, and *dad*.

Figure 15
Activities Using Name Words

- Count the letters in a name. (Some kindergarten children think the length of a name is based on the size of the person.) This not only reinforces the letter names (and beginning capitals) but draws attention to the varying lengths of words.
- Call or cheer the letters in the name, pointing to each letter as it is named. A name cheer can sound as follows: Give me a T! T! Give me an O! O! Give me an M! M! What have you got? TOM!
- Say the letters of the name in a chant or rhythm. Add snapping fingers or clapping to the rhythm to add yet another mode of learning.
- Cut apart the letters in the name and invite the designated child to put them back together.
- Compare each new name with existing names on the word wall. Which word has the most letters? Are there any repeated letters?
- Draw attention to the way the letters are formed. Have the children draw the letters in the air as you instruct them: A *C* is like a big cookie with a bite out of it. A *D* has a straight back and a big round tummy. A *Z* goes across and down and across.
- Give the children paper and crayons and invite them to try to print the letters in the name. Resist the temptation to correct, and do not expect conventional letter formation. Remember, this is time for experimentation.
- Draw attention to rhyming words: Can you think of a word that rhymes with *Bill*? Does *pill* rhyme with *Bill*? Does *Brian* rhyme with *Bill*?
- Create a set of separate name cards for children to sort according to initial letters, number of letters, and/or matching letters.

One kindergarten teacher worried that, with classroom space for only one word wall, the children in her morning and afternoon classes would be confused by seeing other children's names on the wall. The worry was alleviated when one of the children commented "There's Jason on the wall. I know him from day care."

Packages of letter cards in different colors and fonts may be used for matching. Children also can make alphabet letters using play dough, Wikki Stix, and even their own bodies.

Language play should be just that—play. It should be fast paced and fun, with the goal of developing both knowledge and motivation to take an interest in how language goes together. When we integrate language play into all aspects of literacy learning, we demonstrate to children that language is both meaningful and authentic, while developing the skill and will for reading that is essential to building the foundations to literacy.

For Further Reading

Hall, D.P., & Cunningham, P. (1997). *Month-by-Month Reading and Writing for Kindergarten*. Greensboro, NC: Carson-Dellosa. Provides an excellent description of how to use a name wall in the kindergarten classroom.

CHAPTER 12

Honoring Diversity in the Classroom

Most classrooms today represent an incredible diversity of students. In your kindergarten classroom, there may be children who have been in preschool for 2 or 3 years, as well as children who are participating in organized group settings for the first time. Your classroom may contain children with identified physical, intellectual, or emotional disabilities as well as children with exceptional strengths. It will no doubt include children who are already independent readers as well as children who have only marginal oral language skills. In many schools, children of affluence will mingle with children who come to school lacking even basic needs of food, clothing, and shelter. Addressing this diversity is one of the greatest challenges faced by many teachers.

For the majority of children, learning to read and write evolves quite easily and naturally. Children grow up with many opportunities to speak to others and to hear language spoken. As preschoolers, they sing songs and play games that teach them about the sounds of language. They listen to stories and write messages. When they get to school, their emerging literacy is nurtured by classroom opportunities to read and write and learn about letters and words.

Unfortunately, too many children arrive at school without the preschool literacy experiences that enable them to take full advantage of these learning opportunities. Often these are children whose culture is different from the dominant culture of the school. Standard English may not be spoken in their homes. Many are children of poverty.

Children At Risk

All too often, schools make the mistake of identifying children of different abilities as unable to learn or intellectually "slow." In our society, we tend to associate intelligence with verbal ability and richness of experience. As a result, the child who is verbal and articulate, who has had many experiences with print and with life, and whose self-confidence has been nurtured by a secure family, is frequently identified as "gifted." On the other hand, we may overlook the gifts of the child who may not have had the benefit of intellectual and verbal stimulation before school, or who may speak a language other than English. We may label these students as "weak," when their only weakness has been a lack of experience with language and print. It need hardly be said that it is unfair and inappropriate to correlate lack of experience with lack of intelligence.

Unfortunately, children of diversity are statistically at risk of having trouble learning to read and write. These at-risk children represent cultures that are different from the dominant culture of school. Kathryn Au (1993) identifies three factors associated with children of diverse backgrounds: ethnicity (the national or ethnic origin of one's ancestors), class or socioeconomic status, and the language or dialect spoken in the home. This multicultural group includes more than just newcomers to the United States: Americans born of African, Hispanic, and even Native descent are considered "culturally diverse."

Some researchers predict that by the year 2025, 49% of the students in U.S. schools will be children of color (Smolkin, 2000). Yet our teaching population is still predominantly of Caucasian-European background. We as teachers must learn about the diverse backgrounds of our students so that we can be more responsive to them and adapt instruction to their needs. We need to provide these kindergarten children with the supports they need to catch up to their more advantaged peers.

Different Ways of Knowing

Cultural diversity has particular implications for literacy instruction. Shirley Brice Heath's (1983) classic research taught us that different cultures provide different ways of knowing and ways of taking from books. Children from middle-class homes generally succeed in school more easily because their literacy knowledge and practice tends to match more closely what schools and teachers know and do. However, all children come to school with "cultural capital"; that is, a set of values and experiences based on their family lives. We must recognize and honor these ways of knowing as we plan instruction to meet the needs of all children. On the other hand, we cannot assume that all children from a particular ethnic group will be the same in what they know, how they learn, and what they need.

Differing Language Structures

Slocumb and Payne's (2000) research on "cultures of poverty" tells us that oral language patterns also vary by socioeconomic level. Even children whose first language is English may use nonstandard dialects that interfere with their ability to translate conventional letter-sound correspondences. Neuman and Celano (2000) also found that children in impoverished neighborhoods had less access to environmental print. Public signs were more scarce, contained less print, and were frequently obliterated by graffiti.

Children from middle-class backgrounds are accustomed to hearing the formal language structures of school used in their homes. In low socioeconomic-level homes, most language tends to be of casual register. For example, while children in a professional family might be asked, "Would you please pick up the fork you dropped?" children of poverty might be more likely to hear, "Pick 'at up." Within the culture of poverty, language is often sparse, informal, and functional. Slocumb and Payne (2000) suggest "The inability to use formal register places the students from poverty in an oral and written world that they don't understand" (p. 59). Because they don't understand, these students may get frustrated and behave inappropriately. Similarly, teachers get frustrated because their students just "don't get it," in spite of repeated instructions.

In the same way, children of diverse cultures may have different models of using written language. Some may never have seen an adult pick up a pen or a book before they arrived at school; others may see functional literacy in practice (such as filling out forms or signing checks), but never in recreational or informational reading.

Even the words "Once upon a time" do not mean the same thing to everyone. One of the ways we may penalize children of nondominant cultures is in our heavy use of the time-linear story as a literacy tool. For example, some Asian cultures start with the middle of the story, then move to the beginning and the end. In the oral tradition of many African American homes, storytelling begins at the part that may have the most emotional appeal to the audience and ends with observations about the characters and their motives (Slocumb & Payne, 2000). We must remember that our sense of story, like many other arts, is a cultural convention.

Honoring Diverse Backgrounds

We can demonstrate respect for our students' diverse cultural backgrounds by taking opportunities to learn about the different cultures in our classroom through reading and talking to others. By inviting parents into the classroom to share their knowledge and expertise, we honor both their experience and their child's place in the classroom. However, many parents are intimidated by attending school events. Self-consciousness about language proficiency, negative memories of their own experiences in school, and worry about what they will hear about their children all contribute to their discomfort. It is important to involve parents first in events that are social and nonthreatening. When schools invite the community to turkey suppers, pancake breakfasts, and other festive events, parents are more likely to feel comfortable attending more academic events such as assemblies and parent-teacher conferences. And parents who feel welcome in the school are more supportive of its programs and more inclined to collaborate with teachers in their children's education.

There is a common misconception that children with limited experience with print need more systematic, direct instruction in skill development (Allington & Cunningham, 1997). All too often, educators fall into the trap of assuming that children at risk need more "skill and drill" and relegate them to fill-in-the-blanks and other low-level thinking activities. A recent study by Duke (2000) found that first-grade children in low socioeconomic-level schools were offered quite different print environments than their peers in wealthier districts. These children had fewer opportunities to interact with print, to engage in writing, and to read connected text; instead they spent more time engaged in activities such as copying, taking dictation, and completing worksheets (Duke, 2000). As a result, the literacy disadvantage with which these children began was exacerbated by a lack of opportunities for engaging with print and developing positive attitudes toward reading and writing. Meanwhile, their more advantaged peers spent more time engaged in authentic reading experiences, thereby perpetuating what Stanovich (1994) calls "the Matthew effects" (p. 281); in other words, the rich get richer and the poor get poorer.

What At-Risk Children Need

Allington and Cunningham (1997) are two researchers who assert that these children of poverty need, more than any others, a "print-rich, story-rich, book-rich" classroom experience (p. 209). These are the children who depend on school to become literate. Children at risk need daily opportunities and large blocks of time to read and write (Au, 2000; Strickland, 2000). They need to be engaged in meaningful and motivational literacy activities that help them develop positive attitudes toward reading as a life skill. They need purposeful and deliberate instruction in phonological awareness, alphabet letters and sounds, and concepts about print in the context of real reading and writing. They need exposure to many types and genres of books to develop the vocabulary and experiential base that has been lacking in their preschool experiences. They need opportunities to talk and work and problem solve with others. They need teachers who constantly monitor their progress and adjust instruction accordingly. In other words, they need the same good instruction that all children should receive. But they need it even more.

Implementing best practices in the kindergarten classroom will be enough for most students to begin the road to literacy. For the small percentage of children who do not experience success in learning, special interventions and adaptations may be necessary. These interventions should occur with individuals and small groups, not as whole-class instruction, and should supplement the classroom program, not replace it (Allington & Cunningham, 1997). In kindergarten, these interventions may involve small-group discussions to build oral language skills or story reading to reinforce concepts about print, the alphabetic principle, or story structures. It is important that teachers set reasonable and achievable learning goals for their students, and constantly assess and monitor progress toward those goals, so they can plan instruction that scaffolds each student to higher levels of development.

Au (2000) says, "I believe that the success of children of diverse backgrounds in learning to read and write in school depends on classroom teachers...who have the expertise to develop literacy curricula around and for their students and who can embrace the diversity among learners" (p. 45). Good teachers know that there is no single method or approach that will be effective for all children. They have a repertoire of strategies for assessing student progress, implementing a balanced program of instruction, and providing interventions as necessary to take all children to higher levels of development. Ultimately, it is the teacher who makes the difference for all students.

References

Adams, M.J. (1990). *Beginning to read: Thinking and learning about print*. Cambridge, MA: Massachusetts Institue of Technology Press.

Adams, M.J., Foorman, B.R., Lundberg, I., & Beeler, T. (1998). *Phonemic awareness in young children: A classroom curriculum*. Baltimore: Paul H. Brookes.

Allington, R.L., & Cunningham, P.M. (1997). *Schools that work: Where all children read and write*. New York: Addison-Wesley.

Au, K.H. (2000). Literacy instruction for young children of diverse backgrounds. In D.S. Strickland & L.M. Morrow (Eds.), *Beginning reading and writing* (pp. 35–46). New York: Teachers College Press; Newark, DE: International Reading Association.

Ball, E.W., & Blachman, B.A. (1991). Does phonemic segmentation in kindergarten make a difference in early word recognition and developmental spelling? *Reading Research Quarterly, 26*, 49–66.

Bouas, M., Thompson, P., & Farlow, N. (1997). Self-directed journal writing in the kindergarten classroom: Five conditions that foster literacy development. *Reading Horizons, 38*, 3–12.

Braunger, J., & Lewis, J.P. (1997). *Building a knowledge base in reading*. Portland, OR: Northwest Regional Educational Laboratory; Newark, DE: International Reading Association; Urbana, IL: National Council of Teachers of English.

Brewer, J.A. (1998). Literacy development of young children in a multilingual setting. In R. Campbell (Ed.), *Facilitating preschool literacy* (pp. 119–130). Newark, DE: International Reading Association.

Burns, M.S., Griffin, P., & Snow, C.E. (Eds.). (1999). *Starting out right: A guide to promoting children's reading success*. Washington, DC: National Academy Press.

Button, K., Johnson, M.J., & Furgerson, P. (1996). Interactive writing in a primary classroom. *The Reading Teacher, 49*, 446–454.

Cambourne, B. (1988). *The whole story*. Auckland, NZ: Ashton Scholastic.

Casbergue, R.M. (1998). How do we foster young children's writing development? In S.B. Neuman & K.A. Roskos (Eds.), *Children achieving: Best practices in early literacy* (pp. 198–222). Newark, DE: International Reading Association.

Christie, J.F. (1990). Dramatic play: A context for meaningful engagements. *The Reading Teacher, 43*, 542–545.

Clay, M.M. (1975). *What did I write? Beginning writing behaviour*. Portsmouth, NH: Heinemann.

Clay, M.M. (1991). *Becoming literate: The construction of inner control*. Portsmouth, NH: Heinemann.

Cullinan, B.E. (1989). Literature for young children. In D.S. Strickland & L.M. Morrow (Eds.), *Emerging literacy: Young children learn to read and write* (pp. 35–51). Newark, DE: International Reading Association.

Dahl, K., & Freppon, P. (1995). A comparison of inner city children's interpretations of reading and writing instruction in the early grades in skills-based and whole language classrooms. *Reading Research Quarterly, 31*, 51–75.

Dickenson, D.K. (1989). Effects of a shared reading program on one Head Start language and literacy environment. In J.B. Allen & J.M. Mason (Eds.), *Risk makers, risk takers, risk breakers: Reducing the risks* (pp. 125–153). Portsmouth, NH: Heinemann.

Dickenson, D.K., & Smith, M.W. (1994). Long-term effects of preschool teachers' book readings on low-income children's vocabulary and story comprehension. *Reading Research Quarterly, 29*, 104–122.

Duke, N.K. (2000). Print environments and experiences offered to first-grade students in very low- and very high-SES school districts. *Reading Research Quarterly, 35*, 456–458.

Durkin, D. (1966). *Children who read early.* New York: Teachers College Press.

Fisher, B. (1998). *Joyful learning in kindergarten.* Portsmouth, NH: Heinemann.

Forester, A.D., & Reinhard, M. (1989). *The learner's way.* Winnipeg, MB: Peguis.

Fountas, I., & Pinnell, G.S. (1996). *Guided reading: Good first teaching for all children.* Portsmouth, NH: Heinemann.

Freeman, M.S. (1998). *Teaching the youngest writers: A practical guide.* Gainesville, FL: Maupin House.

Furr, J. (1996). *Easy word games: Building language skills through puzzles, hink pinks, rebus riddles, and more.* New York: Scholastic.

Galda, L., & Cullinan, B.E. (2000). Reading aloud from culturally diverse literature. In D.S. Strickland & L.M. Morrow (Eds.), *Beginning reading and writing* (pp. 134–143). New York: Teachers College Press; Newark, DE: International Reading Association.

Gambrell, L.B., & Dromsky, A. (2000). Fostering reading comprehension. In D.S. Strickland & L.M. Morrow, *Beginning reading and writing* (pp. 143–154). New York: Teachers College Press; Newark, DE: International Reading Association.

Gatzke, M. (1991). Creating meaningful kindergarten programs. In B. Spodek (Ed.), *Educationally appropriate kindergarten practices* (pp. 97–110). Washington, DC: National Education Association.

Glazer, S.M. (1989). Oral language and literacy development. In D.S. Strickland & L.M. Morrow (Eds.), *Emerging literacy: Young children learn to read and write* (pp. 16–26). Newark, DE: International Reading Association.

Goswami, U., & Bryant, P. (1990). *Phonological skills and learning to read.* Mahwah, NJ: Erlbaum.

Hall, D.P., & Cunningham, P.M. (1997). *Month-by-month reading and writing for kindergarten.* Greensboro, NC: Carson-Dellosa.

Harste, J.C., & Woodward, V.A. (1989). Fostering needed change in early literacy programs. In D.S. Strickland & L.M. Morrow (Eds.), *Emerging literacy: Young children learn to read and write* (pp. 147–159). Newark, DE: International Reading Association.

Harste, J.C., Woodward, V.A., & Burke, C.L. (1984). *Language stories and literacy lessons.* Portsmouth, NH: Heinemann.

Heath, S.B. (1983). *Ways with words: Language life and work in communities and classrooms.* Cambridge, UK: Cambridge University Press.

Hiebert, E.H., & Raphael, T.E. (1998). *Early literacy instruction*. Fort Worth, TX: Harcourt Brace.

Hoffman, J., Roser, N., & Battle, J. (1993). From the modal to a model. *The Reading Teacher, 46*, 496–503.

Holdaway, D. (1979). *The foundations of literacy*. Sydney: Ashton Scholastic.

Holliman, L. (1996). *The complete guide to classroom centers*. Cypress, CA: Creative Teaching Press.

International Reading Association (IRA). (1997). *The role of phonics in reading instruction*. A position statement of the International Reading Association. Newark, DE: Author.

International Reading Association (IRA). (1998). *Phonemic awareness and the teaching of reading*. A position statement from the Board of Directors of the International Reading Association. Newark, DE: Author.

International Reading Association (IRA). (2000). *Excellent reading teachers*. A position statement of the International Reading Association. Newark, DE: Author.

International Reading Association (IRA) & National Association for the Education of Young Children (NAEYC). (1998). Learning to read and write: Developmentally appropriate practices for children. *The Reading Teacher, 52*, 193–216.

Johnson, T.D., & Louis, D.R. (1987). *Literacy through literature*. Richmond Hill, ON: Scholastic.

Kuby, P., Aldridge, J., & Snyder, S. (1994). Developmental progression of environmental print recognition in kindergarten children. *Reading Psychology, 15*, 1–9.

Lapp, D., Flood, J., & Roser, N. (2000). Still standing: Timeless strategies for teaching the language arts. In D.S. Strickland & L.M. Morrow. *Beginning reading and writing* (pp. 183–193). New York: Teachers College Press; Newark, DE: International Reading Association.

Lesiak, J. (1997). Research-based answers to questions about emergent literacy in kindergarten. *Psychology in the Schools, 34*, 143–160.

Martinez, M., & Teale, W. (1987). The ins and outs of a kindergarten writing program. *The Reading Teacher, 40*, 444–451.

Martinez, M., & Teale, W. (1988). Reading in a kindergarten classroom library. *The Reading Teacher, 41*, 568–572.

Mason, J., Peterman, C., & Kerr, B. (1989). Reading to kindergarten children. In D.S. Strickland & L.M. Morrow (Eds.), *Emerging literacy: Young children learn to read and write* (pp. 52–62). Newark, DE: International Reading Association.

McCarrier, A., Pinnell, G.S., & Fountas, I. (2000). *Interactive writing: How language and literacy come together*. Portsmouth, NH: Heinemann.

McGee, L.M., & Richgels, D.J. (1989). "K is Kristen's": Learning the alphabet from a child's perspective. *The Reading Teacher, 43*, 216–225.

McGee, L.M., & Richgels, D.J. (1996). *Literacy's beginnings: Supporting young readers and writers* (2nd ed.). Boston: Allyn & Bacon.

McGill-Franzen, A. (1992). Early literacy: What does "developmentally appropriate" mean? *The Reading Teacher, 46*, 56–58.

McLachlan-Smith, L. (1993). *Developing literacy in kindergarten: An examination of teachers' beliefs*. Paper presented at the Fifth Annual Meeting of the Australia and New Zealand Conference on the First Years of School, Perth, Western Australia. (ED 37776930)

Miller, L. (1998). Literacy interactions through environmental print. In R. Campbell (Ed.), *Facilitating preschool literacy*. Newark, DE: International Reading Association.

Morrow, L.M. (1997). *The literacy center: Contexts for reading and writing.* York, ME: Stenhouse.

Morrow, L.M., O'Connor, E.M., & Smith, J.K. (1990). Effects of a story reading program on the literacy development of at-risk kindergarten children. *Journal of Reading Behavior, 22,* 213–231.

Morrow, L.M., Strickland, D.S., & Woo, D.G. (1998). *Literacy instruction in half- and whole-day kindergarten.* Newark, DE: International Reading Association.

Nation, K., & Hulme, C. (1997). Phonemic segmentation, not onset-rime segmentation, predicts early reading and spelling skills. *Reading Research Quarterly, 32,* 154–167.

National Association for the Education of Young Children (NAEYC). (1986). A position statement on developmentally appropriate practices in early childhood programs serving children from birth through age eight. *Young Children, 42,* 4–19.

National Reading Panel (NRP). (2000). *Teaching children to read: Reports of the subgroups.* Bethesda, MD: National Institute of Child Health and Human Development. http://www.nichd.nih.gov/publications/nrp/report.htm or http://www.nationalreading panel.org/Publications/summary.htm

Neuman, S.B. (1998). How can we enable all children to achieve? In S.B. Neuman & K.A. Roskos (Eds.), *Children achieving: Best practices in early literacy* (pp. 5–19). Newark, DE: International Reading Association.

Neuman, S.B., & Celano, D. (2000). Access to print in low-income and middle-income communities: An ecological study of four neighborhoods. *Reading Research Quarterly, 36,* 8–28.

Neuman, S.B., & Roskos, K.A. (1992). Literacy objects as cultural tools: Effects on children's literacy behaviors in play. *Reading Research Quarterly, 27,* 203–225.

Neuman, S.B., & Roskos, K.A. (1998). *Children achieving: Best practices in early literacy.* Newark, DE: International Reading Association.

Partridge, M. (1991). *The effects of daily opportunities to draw and write on kindergarten children's ability to represent phonemes in their spelling inventions.* Paper presented at the Annual Meeting of the National Association for the Education of Young Children, Denver, CO.

Peterson, M.E., & Haines, L.P. (1992). Orthographic training with kindergarten children: Effects of analogy use, phonemic segmentation and letter-sound knowledge. In C. Weaver (Ed.), *Reconsidering a balanced approach to literacy* (pp. 159–180). Urbana, IL: National Council of Teachers of English.

Pikulski, J.J. (1998, August/September). Reading and writing in kindergarten: Developmentally appropriate? *Reading Today,* p. 24.

Purcell-Gates, V., & Dahl, K. (1991). Low-SES children's success and failure at early literacy learning in skills-based classrooms. *Journal of Reading Behavior, 23,* 1–34.

Reutzel, D., Oda, L., & Moore, B. (1989). Developing print awareness: The effects of three instructional approaches on kindergarteners' print awareness, reading readiness and word reading. *Journal of Reading Behavior, 21,* 197–217.

Reynolds, B. (1998). To teach or not to teach reading in the preschool...that is the question. In R. Campbell (Ed.), *Facilitating preschool literacy* (pp.155–168). Newark, DE: International Reading Association.

Richgels, D. (1995). Invented spelling ability and printed word learning in kindergarten. *Reading Research Quarterly, 30,* 96–109.

Richgels, D., Poremba, K., & McGee, L. (1996). Kindergartners talk about print: Phonemic awareness in meaningful contexts. *The Reading Teacher, 49,* 632–642.

Rog, L.J., & Burton, W. (in press). Matching readers and texts: Using leveled reading materials for assessment and instruction. *The Reading Teacher.* Newark, DE: International Reading Association.

Roskos, K.A. (1995). Creating places for play with print. In *Readings for linking literacy and play* (pp. 8–17). Newark DE: International Reading Association.

Roskos, K., & Neuman, S. (1993). Descriptive observations of adults' facilitation of literacy in young children's play. *Early Childhood Research Quarterly, 8,* 77–97.

Saskatchewan Education. (1994). *Children first: A curriculum guide for kindergarten.* Regina, SK: Author.

Saskatchewan Education. (2000). *Early literacy: A resource for teachers.* Regina, SK: Author.

Scarborough Board of Education. (1997). *Teaching children to read and write.* Toronto, ON: Toronto District School Board.

Schickedanz, J.A. (1998). What is developmentally appropriate practice in early literacy? Considering the alphabet. In S.B. Neuman & K.A. Roskos (Eds.), *Children achieving: Best practices in early literacy* (pp. 96–106). Newark, DE: International Reading Association.

Schlosser, K., & Phillips, V. (1992). *Building literacy with interactive charts.* New York: Scholastic.

Sipe, L.R. (1998). The construction of literary understandings by first and second graders in response to picture storybook read-alouds. *Reading Research Quarterly, 33,* 376–378.

Slaughter, J.P. (1993). *Beyond storybooks: Young children and the shared book experience.* Newark, DE: International Reading Association.

Slocumb, P.D., & Payne, R.K. (2000). *Removing the mask: Giftedness in poverty.* Highlands, TX: RFT.

Smolkin, L. (2000). How will diversity affect literacy in the next millennium? Response by Laura Smolkin. *Reading Research Quarterly, 35,* 549–550.

Snow, C.E., Burns, M.S., & Griffin, P. (1998). *Preventing reading difficulties in young children.* Washington, DC: National Academy Press.

Stanovich, K. (1994). Romance and reality. *The Reading Teacher, 47,* 280–291.

Strickland, D.S. (1989). A model for change: Framework for an emergent literacy curriculum. In D.S. Strickland & L.M. Morrow (Eds.), *Emerging literacy: Young children learn to read and write* (pp. 135–146). Newark, DE: International Reading Association.

Strickland, D.S. (2000). Classroom intervention strategies: Supporting the literacy development of young learners at risk. In D.S. Strickland & L.M. Morrow (Eds.), *Beginning reading and writing* (pp. 3–22). New York: Teachers College Press; Newark, DE: International Reading Association.

Strickland, D.S., & Morrow, L.M. (1989). Environments rich in print promote literacy behavior during play. *The Reading Teacher, 43,* 178–179.

Strickland, D.S., & Taylor, D. (1989). Family storybook reading: Implications for children, families, and curriculum. In D.S. Strickland & L.M. Morrow (Eds.), *Emerging literacy: Young children learn to read and write.* Newark, DE: International Reading Association.

Sulzby, E. (1985). Children's emergent reading of favorite storybooks: A developmental study. *Reading Research Quarterly, 20,* 458–481.

Sulzby, E., Teale, W. H., & Kamberelis, G. (1989). Emergent writing in the classroom: Home and school connections. In D.S. Strickland & L.M. Morrow (Eds.), *Emerging literacy: Young children learn to read and write* (pp. 147–159). Newark, DE: International Reading Association.

Sweet, A.P., & Guthrie, J.T. (1996). How children's motivations relate to literacy development and instruction. *The Reading Teacher, 49*, 660–662.

Teale, W.H., & Martinez, M. (1987). Connecting writing: Fostering emergent literacy in kindergarten. In J. Mason (Ed.), *Reading and writing connections*. Newton, MA: Allyn & Bacon.

Teale, W.H., & Yokota, J. (2000). Foundations of the early literacy curriculum. In D.S. Strickland & L.M. Morrow (Eds.), *Beginning reading and writing* (pp. 3–22). New York: Teachers College Press; Newark, DE: International Reading Association.

Thomas, K. (1992). Oral language, literacy and schooling: Kindergarten years. *Reading Horizons, 33*, 149–166.

Trehearne, M.P., Healy, L.H., Cantalini-Williams, M., & Moore, J.L. (2000). *Nelson language arts: Kindergarten teacher's resource book*. Scarborough, ON: Nelson Thompson Learning.

Turner, J.C., & Paris, S.G. (1995). How literacy tasks influence students' motivation for literacy. *The Reading Teacher, 48*, 662–675.

Vukelich, C. (1994). Effects of play interventions on young children's reading of environmental print. *Early Childhood Research Quarterly, 9*, 153–170.

Vygotsky, L.S. (1978). *Mind in society: The development of higher psychological processes* (M. Cole, V. John-Steiner, S. Scribner, & E. Souberman, Eds. and Trans.). Cambridge: Harvard University Press. (Original work published 1934)

Weaver, B.M. (2000). *Leveling books K–6: Matching readers to text*. Newark, DE: International Reading Association.

Wigfield, A. (1997). Children's motivations for reading and reading engagement. In J.T. Guthrie & A. Wigfield (Eds.), *Reading engagement: Motivating readers through integrated instruction* (pp. 14–33). Newark DE: International Reading Association.

Yaden, D.B., Smokin, L.B., & Conlon, A. (1989). Preschoolers' questions about pictures, print conventions, and story text during reading aloud at home. *Reading Research Quarterly, 24*, 188–214.

Yopp, H. (1995). Read-aloud books for developing phonemic awareness: An annotated bibliography. *The Reading Teacher, 48*, 538–543.

Children's Book References

Baylor, B. (1987). *Everybody needs a rock*. New York: Aladdin.

Brown, M.W. (1999). *The important book*. New York: HarperCollins.

Browne, A. (1989). *Things I like*. New York: Random House.

Calmenson, S. (1994). *It begins with A*. New York: Hyperion.

Carle, E. (1994). *The very hungry caterpillar*. New York: Philomel.

Carle, E. (1996). *The grouchy ladybug*. New York: HarperCollins.

Chase, E. (1999). *The new baby calf*. Topeka, KS: Econo-Clad.

Ehlert, L. (1993). *Eating the alphabet*. New York: Red Wagon.

Guarino, D. (1991). *Is your Mama a Llama?* New York: Scholastic.

Hitomura, S. (1992). *From Acorn to Zoo and everything in between in alphabetical order*. New York: Farrar, Straus & Giroux.

Hutchins, P. (1989). *The doorbell rang*. New York: HarperCollins.

Hutchins, P. (1983). *Rosie's walk*. NY: Aladdin Books.

Knight, M.B. (1995). *Talking walls*. Gardiner, ME: Tilbury House.

Martin, Jr, B. (1996). *Brown Bear, Brown Bear, What do you see?* New York: Henry Holt.

Neitzel, S. (1989). *The jacket I wear in the snow*. New York: Greenwillow.

Pallotta, J. (1990). *The ocean alphabet book*. Watertown, MA: Charlesbridge.

Pallotta, J. (1993). *The icky bug alphabet book*. Watertown, MA: Charlesbridge.

Seuss, Dr. (1960). *Green eggs and ham*. New York: Random House.

Seuss, Dr. (1963). *Dr. Seuss's ABC*. New York: Random House.

Seuss, Dr. (1963). *Hop on Pop*. New York: Random House.

Seuss, Dr. (1966). *One fish, two fish, red fish, blue fish*. New York: Random House.

Seuss, Dr. (1970). *Mr. Brown can moo, can you?* New York: Random House.

Seuss, Dr. (1974). *There's a wocket in my pocket*. New York: Random House.

Slate, J. (1996). *Miss Bindergarten gets ready for kindergarten*. New York: Dutton.

Thornhill, J. (1988). *The wildlife ABC: A nature alphabet*. Toronto, ON: Grey de Pencier.

Tolhurst, M. (1991). *Somebody and the three Blairs*. New York: Orchard.

Wadsworth, O.A. (1991). *Over in the meadow*. New York: Scholastic.

Ward, C. (1992). *Cookie's week*. New York: Putnam.

Index

Note: Page numbers followed by *f* indicate figures.